Eric

" When you sur
great people, g

Thank you for being one of the great
people on the imYEG Council of Founders
helping innovators turn their dreams
into reality!

Clint

ONE DAY YOU'LL UNDERSTAND

Christopher Micetich

ONE DAY YOU'LL
Understand

AN ENTREPRENEUR'S PATH TO PURPOSE, AUDIENCE, AND VOICE

Published by Advantage, Charleston, South Carolina.
Member of Advantage Media Group.

ADVANTAGE is a registered trademark, and the Advantage colophon is a trademark of Advantage Media Group, Inc.

Printed in the United States of America.

10 9 8 7 6 5 4 3 2 1

ISBN: 978-1-59932-896-6
LCCN: 2018963906

Book design by Megan Elger.

Advantage Media Group is proud to be a part of the Tree Neutral® program. Tree Neutral offsets the number of trees consumed in the production and printing of this book by taking proactive steps such as planting trees in direct proportion to the number of trees used to print books. To learn more about Tree Neutral, please visit **www.treeneutral.com**.

Advantage Media Group is a publisher of business, self-improvement, and professional development books and online learning. We help entrepreneurs, business leaders, and professionals share their Stories, Passion, and Knowledge to help others Learn & Grow. Do you have a manuscript or book idea that you would like us to consider for publishing? Please visit **advantagefamily.com** or call **1.866.775.1696**.

I would like to dedicate this book to the two most important and influential ladies in my life. My wife, Kelly Alexandra Micetich, who has stood by my side through thick and thin, and my mother, who has challenged me to fight for what I truly believe—even though for most of my life, that fight has been with her, I remain forever grateful! Without the love, support and the challenge of these two incredible women, I would not be who I am today.

TABLE OF CONTENTS

ACKNOWLEDGMENTS

My team of supporters, Sameeh Salama, Samarendra Maiti, Lindsay Oligny, and Kirby Wyatt—to name only a few of many—who, behind the scenes, did everything that needed to be done for me to succeed. "When you surround yourself with great people, great things happen." I've been blessed to have the love, support, and faith of so many incredible people, but this particular team of individuals has kept me focused, kept me confident, and given me purpose.

INTRODUCTION

After all these years, I can still see the scenes with crystal clarity. The details remain vivid—as sharp as any 4K TV—though decades have passed.

I'm a young man in these memories—about twenty-five years old, and I'm in a rush to get where I need to go. Who isn't, at that age?

It's 1987 or early 1988, and I'm trying to reach light speed. I know where I want to go—and what I want to become. But to get there, I've got to make an unscheduled stop at my father's office to get his approval on some idea or initiative I feel in my gut is brilliant, perfect, a true game changer.

I'm a hypersonic jet barreling through the office, past his secretary, through the doorway into his office.

Looking back, everything appears as if glued in place. The maps on the walls. The books on the shelves. The photographs in frames. And there's my father's big wooden desk topped with reams and reams of paper reports and research. They're stacked so high you can

1

barely make out my dad's eyes above the paperwork. He's got his glasses perched precariously on his nose—his trademark look. And when I burst into the room, he stops whatever he's doing and turns his attention to me.

I look different in these daydreams than I do today. I actually have hair instead of the sleek look I will embrace in later years. My suits are tight in an attempt to accentuate all the time I'm spending in the gym. I'm a blur of speed and conviction, sprinting into my father's office and catapulting my body into one of the chairs facing his desk.

My dad, who stands at five-foot-six, max, may be shorter than I am, but he commands the room. Ronald Micetich may have been responsible for the creation of tazobactam, a world-class anti-infective that has helped save countless lives over the years, but he never carried himself like a genius or a scientific savior—especially not when I came calling.

He takes off his glasses and leans back, sliding back in his chair at the same time as I lean forward in mine.

I talk and he listens. And I watch him as I'm distilling all my pent-up energy—all the ideas that have formed and buzzed around in my head over the last twenty-four hours. And I see he's absorbing it all. He's not interjecting. He's not wielding his influence or making sure he gets a word in. He's just listening—paying close attention to what I have to tell him, whether it's why we should be hiring someone or letting someone else go for insubordination or moving the business in a new direction.

He's just sitting back listening to my story, waiting for me to finish.

These flashbacks come to me quite often these days, usually when I'm sitting down and counseling other entrepreneurs on how to achieve their particular business aims through my company Brass Dome Ventures. Often they emerge when I'm expressing one of my core business philosophies—that the word *mentor* should be viewed more as a noun than a verb.

I believe that a mentor is something you are, not something you do. If you live your life in a way that allows you to become a role model for others, you are a mentor.

I've found that an entrepreneur's story is often the best way to communicate wisdom. Your personal growth is your own. Your challenges are your own. But in

> *I believe that a mentor is something you are, not something you do.*

relating honestly and insightfully what allowed you to become the person you are today, you can help other budding entrepreneurs examine their own journey.

A successful life, and a successful business life, isn't the result of following a set of prescribed rules. It's about listening to the stories of others and letting them find their own truth in that narrative.

And thus, when I'm sitting across from a potential entrepreneur and I'm trying to explain my thoughts on the word *mentor*—on the importance of seeing it as a noun instead of a verb—I can't help but go back in time to those early years of my career when I'd rush into my father's office and bombard him with ideas and advice and admonitions.

I'd keep talking, and he'd keep listening. When I ran out of steam, he'd never give me instructions, never mentor me—at least not in the sense that he'd tell me what to do. If I kept pushing, all he'd say was "I think you can try that," or "We shouldn't do that."

No lessons were granted. He never showed a desire to control the situation or dictate terms.

In the end, he often gave me the freedom to charge forward when I'd come to some prudent realization, but more often than not, he'd just lead by example, which could be frustrating for anyone who wanted step-by-step instructions—some concrete direction, a recipe for what needed to be done in what order.

Rather than give what was being asked, my father would utter one line that, for many years, I didn't fully understand.

"One day, Chris," my father often said. "One day, you'll understand."

The book you hold in your hands is a chronicle of my own journey, my own path toward *understanding* and coming to grips with what the word *mentor* truly means.

CHAPTER ONE

A Breed Apart

In the beginning, no one believed.

In September 2010, when I announced to my board of directors that I was committed to developing a new bacteria-busting super drug to combat the world's most virulent antibiotic-resistant bugs, the negativity in the room was so thick you could have choked on it.

Friends. Family. Coworkers. Everyone—with the notable exception of my wife, Kelly Alexandra—said it couldn't be done, that I was chasing an absurd dream. They shook their heads. And rubbed the bridges of their noses. And rolled their eyes—some subtly, others with all the delicacy of a ball-peen hammer.

Occasionally, words burst through the incredulity: "*Can't be done, Chris*," they'd say. "*Investors will never buy it. It's too ambitious. Don't be foolish. You'll never make it work. Never. Do you have any idea how many drugs fail?*"

But I didn't listen. And neither should any entrepreneur in a similar situation—especially if you have the vision and willpower needed to transform seemingly impossible dreams into life-changing realities.

I learned that lesson early in life—a pearl of wisdom mined during a childhood playing basketball and navigating a complex family dynamic in Alberta, Canada.

Never let the negativity consume you. Instead, feed on it. Use it like kindling. Let it stoke a fire—and embolden your resolve instead of fracturing it.

But above all else, find the guts to take the shot—because there's no sweeter sound in life than a perfect swish that turns silence into belief.

> *Never let the negativity consume you.*

In my case, redemption came in the early morning hours of December 22, 2014. At approximately 2:01 a.m. I scrawled my signature on a piece of paper and closed, on behalf of my company Fedora Pharmaceuticals, the single largest licensing deal in Canadian biotech history.

We'd done it. As a team, we'd developed nacubactam, a revolutionary beta-lactamase inhibitor that will someday help antibiotics slay even the most resilient of bacteria—and may, in the process, pull in as much as $750 million (US) in milestone payments plus royalties.

Ask any successful business leader or entrepreneur, and they'll have a similar story. Tell us we can't do something, and we'll be compelled, almost instinctually, to defy our critics and push harder toward our goal.

Everybody has their own name for this particular breed of gumption. Here's one of mine: *perseverance.*

I came to this realization less than a year after the close of the deal, when I was sitting with my wife at an elegant awards ceremony in Toronto.

Within months of signing the deal, we were fortunate to begin accepting awards from various organizations, including a rather memorable evening on November 25, 2015, when I was invited to receive a special national citation for entrepreneurial perseverance from Ernst & Young (EY).

Truth be told, I was unaware that such an award even existed before being notified that I'd won it. I'd already won an EY Entrepreneur of the Year award for the Prairies Region in Canada, but now I'd been selected to receive this special national citation by a panel of esteemed judges from across Canada.

Although I've been to a number of award ceremonies in my life, there was something different this time around—something about winning an award for perseverance that struck a deep emotional cord in me.

The whole affair gave me pause. Although it was a black-tie event in a stunning venue, my wife and I had made the trip along with my "right-hand man" and vice president of business development Sameeh Salama. Our children had stayed at home, and for reasons that will become clear later, my mother and my siblings were not in attendance.

So, except for Sameeh, who was like a brother to me, and a few cousins from Toronto, we were alone—just my wife and I—which somehow made it all the more special. As the minutes ticked by toward my speech, I remember feeling a tidal wave of emotion wash over me. It started in my stomach, then sliced into my chest. That word "perseverance" kept echoing in my mind, causing old memories to begin flickering to life.

If you've ever been at an award ceremony like this, you probably understand what I was experiencing. Little vignettes from my past began speeding, quick as a bullet train, before my eyes. They were almost uncontrollable—the borders between the past and the present blurring into one.

I normally don't get nervous at award ceremonies, but as this pent-up spindle of memories began unspooling, a kind of panic began to set in. Would I be able to keep it together when I was handed the microphone? Would I be able to stunt the tears when I looked out over the crowd and locked eyes with my wife, Kelly? And most importantly, could I find a way to say those two simple words— "thank you" —with the clarity and conviction that she deserved?

Walking up to that dais, I felt like one of those awestruck Academy Award winners you see on TV every year. There were too many people to thank and not enough time to do it. So I sped through a list of people I wanted to thank—my parents, my team members, friends and supporters—but as the list inched toward my wife, I could feel tears building. All I could muster was a choked up "thank you" that I directed her way, as I fought the urge to let loose a full-throated, glassy-eyed sob of gratitude.

It all happened so fast—too fast. I remember immediately feeling disappointed in myself, feeling that I'd failed to accurately communicate just how much my wife meant to me. In moments like these, flashbacks of joy and pain can come in equal measure. We'd experienced so much hardship along the way. Hurt. Pain. Suffering. She'd absorbed just as much I had, but had supported me every step of the way.

I realized, right then and there, that this wasn't a "me" accomplishment. It was a team effort—Sameeh, Lindsay, Kirby, Maiti—I knew it was a collective achievement, not a personal one.

When I returned to my seat, I felt humbled and grateful to have the love and support of so many great people. I felt the need to apologize to my wife for not doing a better job of thanking her, but she knew exactly what I was feeling. She knew from the crack in my voice and a few choked-off tears exactly how grateful I was for her. Against all odds, we actually did it.

And at the same time, I felt genuinely humbled, because I realized in that moment that my perseverance was a product not only of my own conviction, but of all the impactful moments, both positive and negative, that I'd experienced up to that moment.

A simple truth came into focus, one that I make a point to communicate to the many entrepreneurs I've mentored in the years since that night: Perseverance isn't so much about proving something to others. It's about proving something to yourself—a vastly different and more difficult endeavor.

Perseverance isn't so much about proving something to others. It's about proving something to yourself—a vastly different and more difficult endeavor.

In all honesty, when I was a child I struggled with this distinction. But what I *did* know from a very early age was that I was different from most of my peers. Leadership qualities don't necessarily emerge early in life, but they did for me, helping to set me on a path toward both great success and painful conflict for decades to come.

※※

If you ever have the chance to sit down with a friend from grade school and exchange stories about your childhood, seize the opportunity. It can be extraordinarily beneficial, no matter your age or professional status.

I once had an old friend recount a forgotten story that was so brutally telling that I've never quite been able to shake it from my memory. My friend, Tom, was a student at our school, Our Lady of Perpetual Help (OLPH) in Sherwood Park. Every recess, a group of us would play tag on the monkey bars. Tom didn't have many friends at the time, so he kept to himself. After keeping our game exclusive for weeks, Tom, the "outsider," one day found the courage to ask a few of our gang if he could play with us.

Shy and alone, he watched as the other kids slowly turned their heads, in almost synchronized unison, toward me.

"Well, what do you think, Chris?" they asked. "Can Tom join us?"

My friend said he was struck—and to some degree still is—by the power I wielded as a kid, how the others hung on my every word. That day I did the right thing and said, "Okay," and Tom instantly became part of our group.

But it pains me to hear that story today. What does that say about a group of kids—or about human nature, for that matter—that they willingly anointed a playground monarch? That day I offered a "yes," but how many kids throughout my life might I have negatively impacted by saying "no"?

What I do know is that I *was* different. Maybe you've had a similar experience in your own life, but the truth is that self-confidence can imbue confidence in others. When properly harnessed, self-assurance spreads just as quickly as fear. And when coupled with a proclivity to take intelligent risks, confidence can be a deeply potent and powerful force for good.

What I didn't realize until I was a teenager was that I was different not only in temperament but in skin color as well. My mother and father emigrated from India to Canada in the late 1950s, moving initially from Saskatoon, Saskatchewan, where my father completed his PhD, to a well-to-do area of Alberta called Sherwood Park. My father's first job was at R & L Chemicals in Edmonton, Alberta, just a twenty-minute drive west of Sherwood Park.

Although derided by outsiders as "Sure-White Park" due to the number of affluent, dual-income white families who lived there, my family was never ostracized. In all honesty, it was a great place to grow up. And when I later had a family of my own, I chose to call Sherwood Park home.

Both my father, a chemist, and my mother, an obstetrics nurse, worked hard while still finding time to be a constant presence in my life and the lives of my three siblings. My mom and dad were, however, strikingly different people.

My mother was a firebrand. She'd grown up in an Anglo-Indian colony with a strict military father and in schools run by Roman Catholic nuns, and thus she carried herself with all the confidence of a British imperial. She would never deign to allow anyone to speak disparagingly of—let alone look down on—any member of her family.

If anything, all the kids around our neighborhood, Fairview Court, looked at her as a protective mother hen. If one of the neighborhood kids got injured, they'd come running to my mother to patch them up with Band-Aids and soothing words.

She was always there for us, never missing one of our sporting events or spelling bees. She had some serious moxie, too. When my older brother, and the oldest sibling of four, Keith, got cut from a basketball team in tenth grade by his coach—who incidentally was a Roman Catholic priest—my mother ripped him for forcing my brother to wake at six o'clock in the morning for two full weeks of tryouts only to cut him *after* he'd made the sacrifice.

All the other parents just accepted such things; my mother saw it as a slight and an injustice—and pounced.

My dad, Ronald, on the other hand, was far more mild mannered. He was the living embodiment of a quiet gentleman. Even more than a decade after his passing, people still come up to me and marvel at how he maintained that reassuring smile of his, even during the darkest of moments. He was selfless and altruistic, and all my siblings and I knew it.

We used to chuckle to ourselves when our mom threatened us with the proverbial, "Wait till your father gets home" line. My father was more the family pacifier than the disciplinarian. I can still see him, hands outstretched in a conciliatory position, telling my mother, "Sheila" —although her birth name was Celine, she preferred Sheila— "just calm down. There's no need to be so upset."

When I was a kid, my dad used to pack his 1967 Buick Wildcat up with all the kids from the neighborhood and take us out for ice cream. We smiled and giggled, and as the ice cream came curling out of giant circular containers, one scoop after another, I was proud to be his son.

It was the kind of man he was, giving almost to a fault. My father had a very calming effect on everyone around him. What people, including my own family, invariably perceived to be weakness and naiveté, I later learned was true strength and wisdom. It's sad that in our society it is far more difficult to offer a few simple words of kindness than to lash out with venom or unwarranted criticism.

My father's ability to see what was genuinely good in people was a rare gift, not a curse. I've learned over the years that when people take advantage of kindness, it is a reflection of *their* own weakness rather than a deficiency of the compassionate soul who has chosen to provide it.

So it would be accurate to say that I had an exceptional childhood. All of my siblings—Keith, Brenda, Debbie—and I felt safe and protected. If there was a dark facet to our family, however, it was that all of us—my father included—fought for our mother's approval.

It wasn't so much about winning her praise—which she didn't believe in doling out anyway—but about avoiding her wrath. The competition to avoid mom's critiques

> *I've learned over the years that when people take advantage of kindness, it is a reflection of their own weakness rather than a deficiency of the compassionate soul who has chosen to provide it.*

became so fierce that it often pit us siblings against each other. This almost gladiatorial battle to claim her love has remained a primitive yearning in all of us as we progressed into adulthood, and, as you'll go on to read, began to directly affect our business endeavors.

Nothing was ever good enough for Mom, and we knew it. Our aim was to try to limbo beneath the punishingly low bar for mistakes that she set for all of us.

To this day, she'd likely argue that it was her unrelenting expectations for excellence that motivated all of us kids to be such high achievers. And she might be partially right. It might have played a role, but at times it also made for a downright stifling environment to grow up in.

The notion that we might want to follow our own passions on our own terms was a foreign concept in our house. In my opinion, all of us felt trapped—almost handcuffed—into living the life our mother wanted us to live instead of the one that we ourselves hoped to pursue.

There's no doubt that my mother truly loved us all and wanted the best for us. The problem was that she felt she was the only one who knew what was best for us—and there was no convincing her otherwise.

My mom was always pushing us to go into medicine or law, professions that she deemed high status enough for her children. I was fortunate that my older brother, Keith, absorbed much of the pressure. I, however, as a middle child, began to assume the role of the resident black sheep of the family, even as a child.

Looking back, it's interesting that my mother both respected and despised this trait in me. She loved that I would stand up for myself, but she had absolutely no tolerance for it when I decided to stand up to her. I was torn. On the one hand, I craved her approval, but on the other, I bristled at the thought of giving up what I wanted in exchange for it.

And yet the fire that burned in my mother was a part of me as well. And I found it extremely useful—looking back, maybe *too* useful—to leverage that toughness and tenacity in school and during my early years in business.

Power plays, after all, don't begin in the boardroom; they begin in the schoolyard. When I was in seventh grade, I got into a pushing match with another kid. I remember verbally fencing with him for a little while, and when he started to lose the battle he decided to call me a "Paki."

Never mind that my lineage stemmed from India, that slur made me realize that I was indeed different (in terms of my ethnic background) than most of the kids around me. Looking back, I could have taken two approaches. My dad's approach would have been to rise above such petty prejudices and parry with a smarter retort.

My mom's approach would have been much different. She would have lashed out with as much fury as she could muster.

I chose, with little hesitation, the latter. I started pounding the kid. The goal was to beat the snot out of him and to ensure that everyone knew to never, ever use the P-word in my presence again.

In that moment, I determined that I'd never be the flight guy; when the chips were down, I'd always be the fight guy.

I earned a reputation, which carried with me for many years, for being willing to fight in the face of any slight. The word around the schoolyard was that you could get in an argument with Chris, but if you wanted to send him into a seething rage, all you had to do was throw around the P-word and it was game on. I had defended myself, but I'd exposed a weakness in the process.

I realize now that the right response would have been somewhere in between my mother's and father's. I had viewed those unwilling to immediately get into a tussle—people like my father—as being weak. I was in constant fight mode, and in some situations, it was invaluable. But as I've gotten older, I've come to see, especially for entrepreneurs and business leaders, that staying in fight mode isn't always the best strategy. The key to success is fighting to protect others as opposed to protecting your own wounded pride.

You have to pick your battles. No one wants to align themselves with a CEO who goes to war over everything. There's too high a price to pay. But people do tend to line up

> *The key to success is fighting to protect others as opposed to protecting your own wounded pride.*

behind an entrepreneur who knows which battles to fight and makes it a priority to protect his own people in the process.

Being called a Paki, however, paid unexpected dividends. It fueled a competitive spirit in me that has never been extinguished. I grew hungrier and more determined to carve out a niche for myself. Although I got good grades, my older brother was viewed within the family as the real scholar-in-training, the one who never disappointed when the honor roll came around. So I decided to pave my own path and shifted my primary focus to athletics.

I played every sport imaginable, but I was intensely drawn to basketball. For me sports were empowering, because I was a good athlete and I craved competition. I still do. Like most business leaders and entrepreneurs, I don't like losing. I don't feel comfortable with the prospect of anyone besting me in a challenge. My wife still shakes her head at the competitive fire that erupts in me when I play a simple board game with my family. I play to win—always.

But I've come to realize that the great skill that can be gleaned in playing sports has more to do with learning how to be a field general. It's the psychological complexities embedded in sports that matter. How, for instance, can you convince others to play very specific roles to the best of their ability, so that a team can become better than its individual parts?

In the end, playing sports is about reaching your potential while developing the people around you. That's a goal best achieved by validating the importance of other people's individual roles on the team— and highlighting how their efforts are invaluable to the end result.

On the basketball court, I'd carefully determine who was the best defender, who was the natural assist artist, who was a beast on the boards. Even back then, I was something of a player-coach.

What's essential, I've found, is that in business, as in sports, someone has to willingly put the fate of the team on their shoulders. I remember in ninth grade being called into my coach's office and being told, "The future of Archbishop Jordan basketball is on your shoulders now."

Never mind that later in life, I learned that all the good players got the exact same talk in the ninth grade. It was the ones who chose to embrace coach's leadership challenge that succeeded—and the ones who shrunk from his gambit that ultimately slid into the shadows.

One game in particular is seared into my memory. After winning the Edmonton city league, we went to provincials in Medicine Hat, Alberta, which is the Canadian version of state finals. A rival team out of Calgary, Viscount Bennett High School, was getting all the media attention and was favored to win by just about all the so-called experts.

It turned out that both Viscount and my team, the supposed underdogs, reached the finals. I remember our coach—his name was Wayne—pulling me aside the night before the championship game and telling me, "I think our road has come to an end, Sky. It's been a good run." My nickname at the time was Sky because I could generate serious elevation.

"I think these guys are too good," he said. "I don't think we have the horses to beat them."

I was enraged. I looked at him with absolute contempt in my eyes, and I told him where he could shove his negativity.

"If you don't think we're going to win, just sit back and enjoy the show," I said. "I guarantee we're going to win that game."

That night, I called a players-only meeting in my hotel room. I remember giving an impassioned speech about how this was our *last* high school basketball game—*ever*. And how we were damn well going to go out on a winning note because this was *the one game* that mattered.

But looking around, I could sense that some of my teammates shared Coach Wayne's skepticism. One guy, his eyes glued to the floor, said he wasn't even sure he wanted to play, because his girlfriend just broke up with him earlier in the day.

I was so outraged at his skepticism—at this complete lack of belief, his selfishness—that I started screaming at my teammates. I remember chastising my recently dumped friend with unexpected fury, telling him that we didn't need any of his personal drama creeping into our locker room. I tore him down to build him back up.

"How can you quit *now*?" I asked him with genuine sincerity and incredulity. "How can you come this far and let some 'girl drama' pull you down? We, your teammates and brothers, need you."

I told my teammates that we were going to win tomorrow and then broke down exactly what we had to do. I wanted them, each with their own individual strengths, to visualize what they had to do for us to get the win. I paired off our five starters against theirs— who, based on all the media attention, were becoming local celebrities. I emphasized all the attention they were getting while reminding my teammates that everyone was ruling us out. We each knew our strengths, we each had an assignment, and we each had one man to shut down from the other team.

Hollywood couldn't have scripted our last high school basketball game any better. Against all odds, we played the game of our lives the following day. Everyone contributed. I lead the game in scoring, keeping their jumper and scorer off the boards and the score sheet. Cliff played the entire game in high gear, cranking the intensity to a level none of us had ever seen. Paul shut down their all-Canadian shooter to single digits. Randy smothered one of their best playmakers like a blanket, generating a handful of turnovers. And Reid grabbed every rebound on both ends of the court while keeping their big man off the glass. Thanks to a total team effort, we took home the championship.

Later, Coach Wayne pulled me aside and told me he knew we wouldn't lose if he kept telling me we were destined to fail.

"I had to light your fire," he told me after the game. "I had to push your buttons."

Knowing who I am today and who he was, I know what he was driving at. It was the first time I ever used the phrase, "It's a 'we' thing, not a 'me' thing." I use it to this very day with regularity. I believe in that idea—that if you surround yourself with the right people and actualize their abilities, great things can happen.

The problem, I soon discovered, was that outside the basketball court, I still felt tethered to my family's expectations. Despite all the passion I may have exhibited with my teammates, I was still allowing my mother's opinions to affect my career decisions. I was still trying to limbo under the bar of criticism rather than leap over it. I still felt the need to prove something to her, instead of proving it to myself.

> *I believe in that idea— that if you surround yourself with the right people and actualize their abilities, great things can happen.*

After graduating from high school, I didn't have a firm grasp on what I wanted to do with my life. But I did know I wanted to play basketball at the next level, as I'd received a number of scholarship offers from area colleges.

I hatched a plan to go to a lesser college and play ball while I took courses that would be transferrable to university. The only wrinkle in my plan was that my parents—both of them, this time—

were having none of it. They were adamant that I begin my tertiary education at a prestigious university.

It was assumed that I'd obtain a university education, then follow in my father's footsteps and become a chemist—blindly traversing the preordained path taken by every other chemist before me. I bristled and pushed back—until my mother gave me an ultimatum: go to university or move out of our house and find someplace else to live.

So I caved, informed the coach at the college where I had already registered of my decision, and headed out to the University of Alberta. It's funny in life how one act of self-betrayal can lead to a lingering state of self-deception. You see it in the business world all the time. Leaders make a decision that betrays who they are and what they've always believed in, and before you know it, the bad decisions start compounding on each other.

I remember going to the University of Alberta and hearing through the grapevine that the university's basketball coach wasn't interested in walk-ons. Even though I'd beat some of the other guys on the team during one-on-one games, I didn't try out for the team. I kept hearing that the coach didn't have any interest in local talent. I let other people's negativity stain my own outlook as to what was possible. I didn't believe enough in myself, so I used all the campus skepticism as a justification to avoid trying out for the team.

It's one of my few regrets in life. Looking back, I know I used my mother as an excuse. I blamed her instead of finding the courage to tackle my own fears. I had two better choices than the one I made. I could have stayed the course with college, taking on student loans and part-time jobs—or I could have muscled up the courage and tried out for the university team, which deep down was what I really wanted to do. I think I would have made the team, but I didn't have the strength to press on, so I'll never know for sure.

I often wonder: How many business leaders and entrepreneurs, at this very moment, are ensnared in a similar cycle of self-doubt? And how many will choose to act rather than capitulate? How many will fool themselves by masking their fear with excuses?

Over time, I've learned that confidence can be a fragile thing. For a while, I'd developed a way to enshroud my confidence in armor, but now I'd discovered a chink in my armor.

How, I wondered, could I find a way to reverse the tide: to stop trying so hard to prove my worth to parents and start proving it to myself instead?

CHAPTER TWO

Being a Mentor Is Not Something You Do, It's Someone You Are

If I were able to slip back through the folds of time and share some words of wisdom with my brasher, more headstrong, and less creaky-kneed college self, I don't think I'd tell him much. I'm a firm believer that there's value to be mined from every single experience, positive or negative, that comes our way.

It's all about the mindset we choose to adopt. If we believe that everything we do has purpose—that there is potential wisdom to be extracted from even the most mundane of tasks—we'll not only be better businesspeople but also better human beings.

Thus, I might offer my younger self only one simple piece of advice: "Do the things," I'd tell him, "that you don't like doing."

That's my advice to entrepreneurs, young and old, to this very day. If you want to avoid failing in business—or in life—don't just hone your strengths, test your weaknesses.

Find a way to put yourself into situations that are a good six paces outside your comfort zone. The more you can fight your natural inclination to avoid discomfort, the better equipped you'll be to deal with real adversity when it comes knocking.

Wisdom is often a by-product of grit. The things that need to be done are precisely the things that *you* need to handle yourself. Seek out value in those moments, no matter your profession, and you'll be surprised just how much you'll unearth.

Wisdom is often a by-product of grit.

This, I grant you, is no easy task. When I was attending the University of Alberta as a young man, I whiled away my first year as if it were one long extended Sunday afternoon.

I didn't want to be there. I didn't want to be saddled with the chemistry-heavy course load my parents had foisted on me. I wanted to be at a different school, studying different subjects, living a different life.

So I committed what I now realize was a cardinal sin: I wasted time.

I dropped classes left and right. And the classes I did take, I didn't bother squeezing any value out of. I just drifted along, guided by neither purpose nor conviction.

I can't tell you the exact moment it happened, but after finishing my freshman year I came to the realization that I was only hurting myself. My attempt to somehow exact revenge on my parents by subverting my own college career wasn't just juvenile, it was counter-productive to my aim of freeing myself from their control.

In life, I've found that some shackles are affixed by other people and some are self-administered. Realizing that you can, in some cases, free yourself is half the battle.

Emerging from these constraints is mostly a product of self-scrutiny. After my first year at university, I knew I had arrived at an important crossroads in my life, so I did what most college students dread most of all: I sat down to figure out what the hell I wanted to do with my life.

Although common sense and cold, hard logic are the best tools for dislodging oneself from a downward spiral, ultimately it's the twin rudders of emotion and gut instinct that most ably guide us back to safety during moments of uncertainty.

In the end, if you feel that something doesn't feel right to you—that you're being pushed against your will—there's a good chance you need to pivot and set a new path.

At the time, my mind kept returning, time and again, to education. I'd always enjoyed teaching and coaching kids. There was something about actualizing latent potential that was magnetic to me.

It was one of the main reasons I was drawn to basketball. If you've ever been on a court when an entire team is firing on all cylinders—pistons pumping, shots dropping, smiles flashing, high fives, butt slaps—you know the feeling of realized potential in action. There's nothing quite like it.

I knew deep down that I wanted more of those feelings—and challenges—in my life. And I figured the classroom might be the best place to find them. So I switched my major to education and got back to my studies, feeling for the first time in my life that I was charting my own course instead of following someone else's directions.

In all honesty, it would have been far easier for me to slog my way through four years at the University of Alberta, earning both my chemistry degree and my parents' approval. That would have been the easy play, as my parents reacted to my collegiate career change with neither empathy nor support. But if wasting one entire year had any benefit, it was that my parents finally seemed satisfied that I was pursuing a degree, any degree, from a reputable university.

I'd been given, however, a sneak preview of what lay at the end of that particular path. I'd watched my oldest brother, Keith, march in lockstep to my parents' wishes and become a doctor. While he was making a good living in a prestigious profession, was well respected, and was a great physician, I could also sense he wasn't really happy.

The challenge for me, as I made this first cautious turn toward independence, was in not overcompensating. Righteous anger can lead to healthy defiance, but an overabundance of defiance can also lead to deep-seated regret.

I see entrepreneurs and business leaders grapple with this problem all the time. How do you quickly shift gears in a way that doesn't lead to overheating and blowing out your engine? How do you keep yourself open to the advice of others at a time when you have to be decisive and commit to your own path?

For me, the answer to that question is inextricably intertwined with the concept of mentorship. You have to be a great judge of character. You need to turn to the right people during moments of doubt or crisis.

Sometimes, when you're young and feel like you've got something to prove, it's easy to forget that you need mentors in your life. But there are questions abound: Whom do you let in? And more importantly, how do you vet their advice? What do you choose to absorb and what do you choose to reject?

It's a cliché to say that you have to understand people—their motivations, fears, strengths, and weaknesses—to become a successful leader. But far too often people have blind spots when it comes to the people they most lean on for advice. Knowing what to take and what to leave is the real challenge.

"Mentor" is an honorable label that you must earn. You cannot call yourself a mentor. You must be called a mentor by someone else. It's not something you do, it's someone you are. I was fortunate in that I'd grown up under the watchful eye of my greatest mentor, my father. But looking back, I'd already absorbed a great deal more from my father at age nineteen than I was willing to admit.

> *"Mentor" is an honorable label that you must earn. You cannot call yourself a mentor. You must be called a mentor by someone else.*

I'd even argue that my decision not to become a chemist was a direct result of me observing my father so closely and intensely. After all, he was a man who loved going to work every day. Whip-smart, perpetually curious, and deeply analytical, he was born to wear a white cotton lab coat. He flat-out loved being a scientist.

And when as a young man you observe the freedom that comes with pursuing your own passions, you can't help but want to feel a similar sense of independence and self-worth in your own life.

It goes without saying, however, that father-son relationships are complicated affairs. Being born an alpha and listening to my mother's incessant criticisms of my father, I often saw my dad as an amazing scientist but a weak man.

Later in life, I'd come to realize that this was a gross oversimplification, but if you were to ask the collegiate Chris Micetich what I thought of my father, I'd probably have praised him as a kind, altruistic man but argued that he was a bit too pliant. The damning adjective I might've used back then would've been "soft."

This was borne, in part, out of the professional struggles that I witnessed him endure. When I was growing up, my dad ran a lab and worked as an adjunct professor at the University of Alberta.

He worked hard to support his family. That much is indisputable. He taught more classes than most full-time professors, all while taking on the additional burdens of attracting outside research funding and running a laboratory. The fact that the university took 40 percent of his funding was, in his eyes, the price he had to pay to do the work he loved.

I see this faulty logic in so many otherwise smart and passionate people. Part of being a good entrepreneur is having the wherewithal to know when your value exceeds your compensation and then taking appropriate action to correct that incongruity. I think my father knew he was underpaid and undervalued, but he didn't have the courage to actually do anything about it.

He feared conflict—to the point where he fell under the dangerous misconception that if he avoided it long enough it would go away. But problems swept under the rug don't disappear over time, they only build and calcify.

When I was in high school, my dad got blindsided by an unexpected career setback. In an extraordinarily myopic and shortsighted strategy, the government of Canada, via the Crown Corporation, decided that the province of Alberta should divert the entirety of its research funding to oil and gas development.

In an instant, the province's pharmaceutical industry dried up. My father's colleagues immediately fled Alberta for posts at large pharmaceutical companies outside of Canada. But my dad stayed, not wanting to uproot his wife and children.

I saw the next chapter of my father's career play out firsthand during my high school and college years when I worked in his lab during the summers. I might not have been enthralled with chemistry, but I was intensely interested in watching my dad in action.

He was an idea man with an insatiable curiosity and drive to explore the unknown and solve real-world problems. In addition to voraciously consuming peer-reviewed medical journals at work, he enjoyed reading science fiction books and watching James Bond movies. The prospect of transubstantiating an idea into something tangible was thrilling to him.

When, for example, all of his colleagues fled Alberta, he turned his attention to raising research funds from Japanese companies, what was then an unusual plan for a Canadian chemist.

The nonbelievers said his plan would never work. But when he flew to Japan, an aggressive medium-sized company named Taiho Pharmaceuticals immediately recognized my father's talent. Within weeks of their initial meeting, Taiho representatives flew back to Canada, met with my father, and signed onto a funding deal with him.

Whenever someone says something—a phrase, a maxim, an idiom—that strikes a chord in you, I urge you to write it down.

Whenever someone says something—a phrase, a maxim, an idiom—that strikes a chord in you, I urge you to write it down. I wish I'd cataloged more of my father's little adages, but some are so indelibly branded into my brain that they've become part of my vocabulary. Here's an important one: "The difficult," he used to say, "we'll do at once; the impossible will take a little longer."

Throughout my father's career, he was constantly being told he wouldn't survive—that he wouldn't be able to get outside research funding, that he could never create his own company, that he could never create new medications that outperformed the current ones. He proved them all wrong.

In terms of ascribing to the belief that the difficult is done at once and the impossible takes a little longer, my father remained good to his word. The majority of my father's attention was focused on complex compounds called beta-lactamase inhibitors. These are extremely difficult compounds to synthesize, as their aim is to weaken antibiotic-resistant bacteria.

Thanks to the overuse of antibiotics, bacteria have evolved defense mechanisms to thwart the effectiveness of those same antibiotics. Beta-lactamase inhibitors are used in conjunction with antibiotics to inhibit the activity of enzymes that degrade these antibiotics, thus allowing the antibiotic to once again become effective and kill the bacteria.

Beta-lactam chemistry is extremely complex, so there are a limited number of companies in the world that can claim to be experts. Taiho, which was primarily focused on cancer drugs, saw my father's expertise in beta-lactamase chemistry as a way to create new drugs to battle the infections that cancer patients often pick up in hospitals while they receive treatment.

The problem for my father was, of course, that there are a host of other obstacles to bringing a drug to market besides simply synthesizing it in a lab. When my father began developing a beta-lactamase inhibitor in the early 1980s that showed great promise, he learned that a rival large pharmaceutical firm had beaten him to patenting their lead compound. Taiho tried to negotiate a deal with this company but was ultimately unsuccessful.

My father was crushed, but he didn't allow it to deter him from doing what needed to be done.

So what did he do? He went back to the drawing board for Taiho, worked around the patents, and came up with an even better and more viable compound. It was that compound that eventually became tazobactam, which is now, in combination with piperacillin, the global drug of choice for treating difficult infections—so much so that it generates sales of $1 billion per year.

Unfortunately, the fact that my father invented tazobactam—his name is on the patent—didn't guarantee him that he'd earn what he deserved from his discoveries. I always felt he got a raw deal from Taiho. My father never saw a cent in royalties and never complained about it. Once he discovered the drug, Taiho successfully handled the clinical trials and then licensed it off to a different pharmaceutical company to sell it, making untold millions. Had my father been a better businessman, I feel my family's financial fortunes would have been much different.

But there's no doubt that my father's work ethic inspired everyone around him. No matter what he worked on, he found a way to do things quicker, better, and more cost effective than the big pharmaceutical companies he was competing against. He taught me, from a very early age, that the little guy could win. That if you got in the game and competed, good things could happen.

That was an important lesson, but in some ways my father's lack of success in his business dealings was equally instructive for me as his scientific breakthroughs and personal ethos. There are a number of lessons I simply wouldn't have developed on my own had I not observed my dad's mistakes.

After years of being told by the University of Alberta that there was not enough money in the budget to offer my father a full-time tenured professor position, the dean of the faculty of pharmacy and pharmaceutical sciences finally approached my father in the spring of 1986 and informed him that he had a position for him.

There are a number of lessons I simply wouldn't have developed on my own had I not observed my dad's mistakes.

Because the dean was going away on vacation, he asked my father what would prove to be a career-changing question: "Do you need to sign your paperwork now or can it wait until I return from my holidays?"

My father, always deferential to authority, told the dean, "No problem. I've been waiting for ten years. Surely I can wait a few more weeks."

You can probably surmise what came next. Over the dean's holiday, the university's budget was cut, forcing the dean to tell my father that the position he'd been offered earlier was no longer available.

After my father was passed over, yet again, for a full-time position as a professor, I knew he was enraged, but he mostly kept it inside.

Even someone as deferential to hierarchies as my father can only get trampled over so much before they're forced into action. Why, he wondered, should I keep paying the university 40 percent of my research dollars, teaching more classes than full-time professors, introducing international contacts, particularly from Japan, to the university, all in exchange for the paltry benefits that come with being an adjunct professor, including the challenges of having to financially support myself?

My father, in a bold move for someone of his temperament, decided that he could roll the 40 percent overhead that the university had been pocketing from his deal with Taiho into a new joint venture company away from the university while maintaining his adjunct professor status. My father proposed starting a new company to Taiho and bringing along a few of his trusted chemists.

Having seen what my father could do while splitting time between research and teaching at the university, Taiho was thrilled at the news. The only thing better than a part-time Dr. Micetich was a full-time Dr. Micetich.

At the time, I had no indication that our paths would soon converge. During college, I'd been watching all this from afar. After graduation, with my teaching degree in hand, I was dead set on slipping out from under my parents' shadow. So I took a job teaching a split fifth/sixth grade class at Colchester Elementary in Sherwood Park.

I was twenty-three years old and green as could be. But I was organized, committed to the job, and excited by the prospect of time spent in a classroom.

I remember immediately being surprised at the negativity that pervaded our staff room. There was a loud, vocal group of teachers who flat out didn't want to be there. They nitpicked and complained about everything every chance they could. The fuel for their fire at that time was government legislation moving all smokers in Alberta either outside of buildings or into separately ventilated rooms to protect the nonsmokers from breathing in secondhand smoke. Being an old school without the budget to renovate a smokers' room and being a nonsmoker all my life, I recall "fondly and smugly" watching several angry teachers huddled in their vehicles on recess breaks with frosted windows of their cars filled with smoke. I'll confess that at that point in my life, I'd yet to adopt my father's "empathy for all" philosophy.

Some of my fellow teachers were at the tail end of their careers. Others were beaten down from years spent in the classroom. And still others had come to the sad conclusion that they weren't cut out for teaching, but didn't have the courage to pursue a different career.

It was at Colchester, of all places, that I began thinking about the indispensable role that an organization's culture plays in its ultimate success. In order to cultivate the right work environment, you need to define your culture as concretely as possible.

If you're building a young company or reorganizing an established one, avoid platitudes. Just because a particular philosophy works somewhere else doesn't mean it's going to work for your company. It's not a one-size-fits-all equation. Different employees, different business challenges, and different business goals all demand very different cultural values.

If you're building a young company or reorganizing an established one, avoid platitudes.

In the end, when it comes to culture building, you have to create the kind of culture you would want to be a part of yourself. To this very day, I would take a lesser scientist who meshes with my culture over a better-skilled chemist who doesn't fit. In the end, all it takes is a few bad seeds to bring down a whole group.

Although my views on corporate culture would sharpen and gain texture in the years to follow, I realized that negativity can spread through an organization like a virus. It's a ripple effect. If you let negative people hang around an organization long enough, they'll prey on the weakest among them. Complaints lead to frustrations. Frustrations lead to anger. Anger causes a dip in productivity. And if you string enough dips in productivity together, the whole system gets thrown out of alignment.

As much as I enjoyed working with my students, I found myself being asked by my principal to help him deal with fellow teachers. What he wanted more than anything else was advice on how to lead. He was a good guy who wanted to stay positive, but he found his optimism crushed under the weight of his teachers' negativity.

I became, for lack of a better term, a liaison between the principal and his teachers. When I wasn't teaching my class or running intramural sports programs, I was being asked to help change the culture of our little school in Sherwood Park.

It was my high school basketball team all over again—except this time I was dealing with disgruntled teachers and overworked high school administrators.

In the end, I've found that you've got to turn your attention to the people who are worth saving. Many of the teachers at our school were upbeat people who were dealing with personal problems. Those are the people who could be converted. Personal trauma or in-the-moment stress is no grounds for firing, but a scheming ne'er-do-well who's committed to fomenting chaos is deserving of a pink slip as fast as you can muster it.

> *You've got to turn your attention to the people who are worth saving.*

The problem for my principal, however, was that he didn't have the power to terminate the people who'd never change—the teachers who relished the negativity and made sure it spread like wildfire through the school. It is very difficult to remove a teacher under the Alberta teachers' union, so I felt very sorry for him. However, at the same time, there were many things he could have done to create and communicate his desired culture than reprimand those not buying into his system. It all comes down to one thing: leadership.

As a business leader, you should have zero tolerance for such behavior. Be unyielding, because as we shall see, once certain people sense weakness, they are prone to switch from dissent to actual damage.

It's all about establishing clear guidelines as to what's acceptable and what's not. Show your authority, and then create open lines of communication that ensure the malcontents get the message that it's your way or the highway. Be a good parent. Treat your employees like family, but make sure those who stray feel the repercussions of those actions. Tough love is the right love.

At the time, these views were just beginning to come into focus, as I was still coming to grips with how much responsibility I'd been handed in a single year. The year was 1987. I figured I'd stay at Colchester for a while and continue to further cultivate my teaching and management skills.

It was right around this time that I got a call from my dad. He needed my help. He'd just completed a joint venture with Taiho and launched SynPhar Laboratories Inc., and he wanted to know if I would be willing to become his director of operations and help him build his business.

I was a bit circumspect. Did my father genuinely want my help or were my parents (i.e., my mother) just dragging me back under their control and away from a profession they never felt was up to their standards? Cautiously I accepted, thinking I would help my father through the summer, then go back to teaching in the fall. The opportunity turned out to be far too great, though, and after a year of listening to smoking teachers complain, I decided a more permanent career change was in the cards.

"Here," I said to myself, "is the chance I've been waiting for. Not only can I win my family's approval but sweep in and orchestrate the very changes that my principal at Colchester was unable to do." The timing was great, and I was "perfect" for the job, or so I thought.

Feeling a bit puffed up and overconfident, I said yes without hesitation, having no idea of the complexities that awaited me on the other side of that decision.

CHAPTER THREE

The Night Superman
Lost His Cape

In the summer of 1987, I thought I knew it all.

When you're a twenty-three-year-old professional, one year removed from college, it's easy to overestimate the power of fresh ideas and to underestimate the value of the men and women who put those ideas into action.

It seems so obvious to me now. You get what you give. Valued employees deliver valued results. CEOs can give lip service all they want to the cult of personality—to the notion that visionary ideas can change the landscape of an industry. But those who fall prey to the temptation that they can do it alone—that they can push boundaries with a disgruntled, unmotivated workforce—are telling themselves a caustic lie.

When I joined my father's company, SynPhar Laboratories, in 1987, I really did think I could do it all. I figured I had to. My list of responsibilities as director of operations ran the gamut from overseeing recruiting and human resources to handling finances and strategic planning.

I had a script all laid out. I was going to play the role of Atlas, the titan who'd shrug and then hoist the entirety of my father's company onto my shoulders.

I'd just spent a year building bridges between the faculty and administration at Colchester Elementary in Sherwood Park, where I'd witnessed how the negativity of a vocal minority could consume the good intentions of so many. I figured that I'd be the hammer and the strength, the superhero who swooped in and saved the day, granting my father all the riches and attention he so rightly deserved.

And that my family—whose validation I still secretly coveted—would finally understand my true worth.

But you know what they say about the best laid plans.

When I walked into my father's company on day one, I found myself surrounded by scientists. It was like a bad flashback. It was my freshman year of college all over again. The lab coats. The beakers. The pocket protectors. Here they all were. *Again.* The specters of my old university chemistry professors come back to haunt me.

Truth be told, I stayed more than an arm's length from them in the early going. I didn't forge connections; I didn't seek common ground. I didn't do any of the things I'd done on the basketball court or at Colchester Elementary. I stiff-armed them instead of embracing them. I'd already convinced myself that there was no time for so-called team building.

"These are the science guys," I told myself. "I'm the business guy. How much time do I really need to spend with them?"

After all, I was too busy fuming over what I perceived to be the passive-aggressive animus coming from Taiho, our Japanese business partners.

When I'd flown to Japan, I assumed I'd make a miraculous splash. Surely, they'd see the fighter in me right out of the gate. All my ideas, which crackled in my mind's eye like a fireplace in January, would prove irresistible. I'd rework budgets, soak up new funding, and give my father all the resources he desired.

Only it didn't play out that way at all. In Japan, youthful passions aren't as appreciated as they are in North America. If anything, youthfulness is shunned. It's experience—the wisdom of one's elders—that's shown the greatest deference.

So in the beginning, I felt wholly disrespected. There was something about the way Taiho management seemed to stare right through me, as if I were as transparent as a sheet of glass, that frayed my every nerve.

Worse yet, no one seemed willing to delve into the nitty-gritty details that I wanted to discuss during budget meetings.

I was guilty of a common sin that so many young entrepreneurs commit early in their careers. I tried to seize respect instead of earn it. I think the Japanese could sense as much. They knew that I was trying too hard to prove that I was confident and capable, when what I really needed to do was focus on proving that to myself.

I remember regularly complaining behind closed doors to my father that our Japanese representatives were too old, too set in their ways, too skeptical. My father would

> *I was guilty of a common sin that so many young entrepreneurs commit early in their careers. I tried to seize respect instead of earn it.*

always let me vent; he'd always let me get what I was feeling off my chest.

He'd just nod his head, let the silence fill the air, and then say, "One day you'll understand." He'd tell me to be patient—to look for the benefits I might not be seeing.

It wasn't easy being patient, especially given what I considered to be some of the more unnerving distractions inside the company. Two of our lead chemists, for example, were constantly at war with each other. Although of equal competence, they were polar opposites. One loud, one soft spoken. One overtly opinionated, the other a pure diplomat.

I used to tell my dad, almost weekly, that we had to fire one of the two and promote the other. I was convinced they simply couldn't coexist in the same company.

But where I saw only conflict, my dad saw competition. He'd treat both of those men as equals. He'd be kind to them, even when they were embroiled in their petty little squabbles. He'd be patient.

And you know what? They made each other better.

Both of them wanted to prove themselves to him so badly that they'd burn the midnight oil trying to stay a step ahead of the other.

Later, when we were hiring junior chemists, a light bulb went on in my head. I started to realize that some of the chemists we were interviewing were going to work well with one chemist director and some were better suited for the other. Each team had its own individual strengths, but in the end we needed both in order to thrive.

During my early years at SynPhar, I did everything I was asked to do. In all honesty, I probably did what in another company would have been asked of four people. But looking back, I don't think I performed my duties as ably as I could have. I was too confident. Too authoritative. Too shortsighted.

All that changed, however, when I answered the phone in the early morning hours of December 22, 1989, and heard a familiar voice.

At the time, I'd been dating a woman named Laura. She was an attractive young woman, inside and out, with a truly kind heart. We hit it off right away as friends. She was a capricorn, very stubborn but a pillar of emotional strength. I liked being around her, and when it became apparent that the feeling was mutual, we started dating. And we continued dating as I went to teach at Colchester and then to work at SynPhar, while she took a job teaching at Uncas Elementary.

One afternoon while teaching her first-grade students, she was running backward during a physical education class at her school. While backpedaling, she quickly turned her head to offer directions to one of her students and felt a sharp pain spring up like a dagger into the back of her head.

Then came a nagging headache—throbbing and steady. Laura was tough. She endured this for several days, then decided to go see a doctor. The doctor diagnosed her injury as a pinched nerve, wrote her a prescription for some muscle relaxants and sent her on her way.

A few days later, at three o'clock in the morning on December 22, I received a distraught call from Laura's mother, that familiar voice, informing me that the paramedics were taking her daughter to the hospital. She'd heard Laura screaming and had run to the bathroom and found Laura sitting on her bathtub ledge, unconscious, leaning on the wall just across from the toilet.

There was cause for concern. In a cruel twist of fate, Laura's grandmother had passed away in the very same home, sitting in the very same spot on the edge of the bathtub with her head leaning against the wall. Laura's mother had found her there, and now, years later, she'd found her own daughter in the same position.

I was at the hospital by the time the ambulance arrived. I knew one of the paramedics, Bruce, who'd transported her, so I went to him for an early diagnosis. He said that by the look of things, it appeared to be a drug overdose.

"Impossible!" I said. I *knew* that was impossible. Laura didn't do drugs. Didn't smoke. Didn't even touch alcohol.

We waited as Laura was quickly wheeled into the hospital for a series of tests. Then, at around ten o'clock, a neurosurgeon appeared in the waiting room.

Judging by his forced, unnatural eye contact, I knew something was very, very wrong.

He informed us that Laura had suffered a cerebral aneurysm. Showing about the level of compassion and humanity you'd expect from a tax auditor, he informed us that Laura was brain dead. Almost immediately, even before Laura was gone, a transplant team asked us if we were open to donating her organs—as if her dying was just a formality, a foregone conclusion. And Laura did die soon after, from complications of the aneurysm.

My Laura, in short, was gone.

No words can describe how stunned we were—the pain, the panic, the confusion. I wanted to deny reality. I wanted to believe I was caught in some bad dream and that I could wake up. But there was no pinching myself out of it.

When her mother asked what I thought about donating Laura's organs, I didn't hesitate. I knew that a few floors away in the same hospital, Laura's father was on dialysis. He needed a kidney, and there was no doubt in my mind that Laura would have wanted her death to help bring some modicum of solace to her father's life.

Eventually he would receive one of Laura's kidneys, which kept him alive for many years. But I can still remember a strange feeling wash over me days later, when I was told that Laura's retinas had gone to another woman and that her lungs had been implanted in a patient running out of time.

I realized that some people have the ability to save lives—both in life and after death.

Laura was one of those people.

When Christmas arrived a few days later, it didn't come bearing peace and light. All I felt was anger and resentment. I held a grudge against God for years afterward, refusing to set foot inside a church or so much as listen to a Christmas carol.

> *I realized that some people have the ability to save lives—both in life and after death.*

I remember being dragged begrudgingly to Hawaii that January by a friend, only to come back feeling completely hollowed out inside.

I felt as barren and helpless as the winter wasteland around me. The leafless trees, the bitter winds, the bleak gray skies. That was me—both inside and out.

To make matters worse, I couldn't focus at work. I couldn't eat. I couldn't sleep. I just had no interest in doing anything. A wave of people—friends, family, coworkers—came rushing to my aid. They wanted to lift me up. Help me. Inspire me. Their outpouring of support was incredible, but I wasn't ready to accept it.

I knew I had a choice to make. When tragedy enters your life, you can either roll into a ball and make justifications for your bitterness, choosing to become—and stay—a victim. Or you can do the harder thing, the right thing. You can use your trauma to better yourself and those around you. You can look for the lessons hidden beneath the pain.

I wasn't ready to do the hard thing yet. The psychological toll was just too great. Here, after all, were people offering precisely the solace and guidance I thought I'd been born to offer. I'd spent my whole life hoping to leverage my leadership skills to help others who needed comfort. And now, here I was, in desperate need of *their* support, feeling an enormous amount of gratitude for it and an appreciative understanding of the responsibility that comes with providing it.

One of my favorite lines, borrowed from the 2002 *Spider-Man* movie starring Toby McGuire, is when Uncle Ben is driving Peter Parker to the library and says: "With great power comes great responsibility." When I investigated this expression, I found it came from a paraphrase of the Bible: "To those who are given much, much is expected." I never really knew why that particular line struck such a chord in me until that moment. From that day forward, I viewed my leadership skills as a gift that came with great responsibility. As an entrepreneur, that line changed me. It gave both Spider-Man and myself genuine purpose.

The truth of the matter is that I had trouble coming to grips with the fact that nothing—and I do mean nothing—I could have done would have saved Laura. You'd think that being freed of any responsibility for Laura's death would have helped me, perhaps scrubbing my conscience of any potential guilt. But it was quite the opposite.

I'd always lived my life with the assumption that I could control my own destiny—that I could will success into existence, whether on the basketball court, in the classroom, or in the boardroom. And now I realized that in order to persevere I had to relinquish control. I had to do something I was unaccustomed to doing: I had to put my faith and trust in others.

This realization crystalized a few months after Laura's death, when my receptionist told me a harrowing story about a family from her church. They'd been caught in a deadly farm fire. The mother and one of her children had been badly burned, and one of her children tragically perished in the accident.

I heard the story on the news, but listening to my receptionist relay the heartbreaking details changed my outlook on my own grief. I stopped feeling sorry for myself that very moment.

After all, how could I keep wallowing in self-pity when a nearby family had lost virtually everything? Perspective is a powerful thing. To this day I draw strength from the fact that no matter how rough things get in my own life, there is someone, probably not too far away, suffering through something far more debilitating. I wasn't alone. All I had to do was look around me to recognize that.

It's strange how you can have your eyes open and still be blind to your own reality.

During my early days with SynPhar, I remember thinking that my dad wasted too much time on trivial things. He used to bring all his employees together for a morning meeting, where we'd share our thoughts and schedule for the day. Often we had little to say, but

It's strange how you can have your eyes open and still be blind to your own reality.

that didn't bother my father. It was important to him to set aside some time before all of us went on with our day to raise concerns and voice opinions as a group.

After losing Laura, I stopped perceiving these meetings as a waste of time. I recommend that all entrepreneurs, no matter how busy, develop some sort of ritual that mimics the intimacy and openness of their family dinner table at home. Those kinds of meetings, believe me, can heal very deep wounds.

I'd always believed in the importance of mentorship, but now I began to understand the power of friendship. I started letting people help me, and I discovered how much I enjoyed their company. Some became more than coworkers; they became lifelong friends.

In talking with my father's scientists, I found that they respected the fact that I'd spent *some* time in chemistry labs in college.

Science, after all, is an endless cycle of bold attempts and crushing failures, with a little success mixed in between. So the fact that I hadn't made the decision to soldier on and get my chemistry degree was viewed as perfectly acceptable to my father's scientists.

I encourage all business leaders, especially those entering unfamiliar industries, to be as honest about their ignorance to their subordinates as possible. If you can spend some time around the men and women who do the work, gleaning some core concepts and the language necessary to communicate what they do to the outside world, that's pretty much all your employees demand from you.

To this day, I'm a fish out of water in a chemistry lab. I'm always concerned about what not to touch, what not to lean on, what I'm going to knock over. It's like watching my mom make rice and curry; it's a marvel to watch, but I'm not built to do it myself.

But if you watch and listen, you'll nevertheless begin to understand.

For me, the ability to translate something as simple as how a rotary evaporator or a mass spectrometer works in simple language showed a willingness to enter and respect the scientists' day-to-day professional lives. Stick around your people long enough—spending time, as I've recommended before, outside your comfort zone—and you'll soak things up.

Eventually I got to the point where I could smoothly discuss everything from purification processes to classes of chemical compounds. But I never made the claim that I knew as much as the scientist who did the work.

My standard line today is, "Look, I'm not a chemist, but I've run a chemistry-based company for thirty years. I consider myself a businessman working in a world of chemists." Outsiders and insiders respect that kind of candor, as it shows you're not trying to be their equal, but rather their champion.

As I made this turn, I was fortunate to find I had a champion within Taiho's ranks: Satoru Nakagami, the head of Taiho's international division.

Mr. Nakagami was not your typical Japanese businessman. He spoke English fluently, had studied Arabic in school, and showed no reticence in speaking his mind. In Japanese culture, it's not uncommon for business leaders to avoid endorsing even the simplest of solutions out of fear that they might contradict their colleagues' wishes and feelings.

With Mr. Nakagami, everyone knew exactly where he stood. He was extraordinarily transparent and honest. Westerners appreciated his candor, but many of his peers resented it.

As someone who could never be charged with holding back ideas, I caught Mr. Nakagami's eye. I quickly became his protégé, but also his friend. We'd regularly go golfing together, during which the wise sensei would instruct his young apprentice how things really got done in Japan.

I did a lot of listening, which is something I fear too many entrepreneurs who seek international partnerships fail to do these days. I began, for example, to understand the importance and power of "saving face" in Japanese society, an unwritten code of honor that says you should never do anything that brings discomfort, let alone shame, to your coworkers or superiors.

When dealing with Taiho, I learned to avoid ever putting a high-ranking businessman into a position where he or she had to make a decision on the spot.

It was a game-changing insight. I realized I'd been negotiating our budgets in wholly ineffective ways. Springing new ideas on an unsuspecting audience was the wrong tack to take. Instead, I started introducing new ideas to key players before the actual meetings.

These friendly pre-meeting get-togethers sped negotiations up exponentially, to the point where the meetings themselves became rubber stamps on decisions that had been worked out ahead of time in private.

With my dad being confrontation averse, he took a backstage role in these negotiations, which allowed me to take center stage. My ability to understand the rituals and procedures of Japan's business culture didn't soften the forcefulness of my positions, but they did add texture to them.

I began to form my own definitions of "honor" and "respect," words often thrown around by people who've never taken the time to consider what they actually mean. I learned that when you give your word to do something, you shouldn't need a contract to enforce it. All that should be required is trust coupled with a handshake.

During negotiations, I found that it was in my best interest always to be direct. Right off the bat, I'd say precisely what we needed and why we needed it. I learned not to dance around the sore spots. That was my way of showing respect: sharing what my issues were so that the other side could do the same.

Some people are under the false impression that if you express what your needs are immediately, the other side will take advantage of those disclosures. I'm sure there are some situations where this is true. But if you've taken the time to establish a rapport with someone and you've projected a positive and upbeat attitude, you're less likely to create fissures that will lead to irreconcilable differences.

If you can mold a win-win proposal, usually the person on the other side of the bargaining table will take it. And you'll find yourself with a new ally.

The problem, of course, especially in negotiations, was that my father believed everyone was his ally, when in some cases they were actually his enemies.

Trust is a fine quality, but only in moderation. Although my father and his group of scientists were delivering amazing compounds to Taiho, including a second success-ful nonsteroidal anti-inflammatory drug called Zosyn, my father received no royalties as the result of these developments.

If you can mold a win-win proposal, usually the person on the other side of the bargaining table will take it. And you'll find yourself with a new ally.

My father formed SynPhar Laboratories as a joint venture with Taiho. The Japanese owned 80 percent, and my father only 20. Had my father received even a minuscule 2 percent royalty for tazobactam from Taiho, he and his family would have received $20 million a year. He knew this, and the Japanese knew this, but my father didn't have the courage to go to the negotiating table to get what he deserved.

In all honesty, he feared doing what it would have taken to sign a good deal. He didn't believe in the golden rule of entrepreneur-ship: nothing ventured, nothing gained. He incorrectly assumed that other people would take care of his interests, instead of the real truth: every entrepreneur has to take care of their own.

Thus, my father didn't sense backside pressure the way you should as the CEO of a company. During the late 1980s and into the early 1990s, when Taiho was happy and we were delivering like gangbusters, my father didn't have any cause for concern. But by the mid-1990s, when senior people within Taiho started retiring, he underestimated the potential danger of transitional moments, even as two of our new employees—a Japanese-speaking employee from Saskatchewan and an in-house lawyer—began orchestrating a clandestine campaign to take over our company.

It proved to be more than a mere rumor when an actual copy of a letter sent from our two schemers to Taiho president Yukio Kobayashi came to my attention. They didn't know that I'd intercepted the message, but now I was well aware of their intentions.

The letters, filled with intimate complaints and slanderous comments about my father and me as well as a list of suggested replacements for my father, were all right there in black and white. To add more salt to the wound, their suggested replacement was the same dean of pharmacy who had rescinded the job offer to my father years earlier. To say I was shocked would be an understatement. Thoughts and flashes of anger bolted across my mind in rapid-fire succession: tazobactam ... Zosyn ... my father's life ... his work ... the decision to hire these traitorous employees. And as for trust, loyalty, friendship, appreciation ... all that seemed to be worth nothing now.

I knew this couldn't stand. I marched as quickly as I could into my father's office and said we had to fire the two conspirators immediately. But my father showed trepidation in doing anything of the sort. He was paralyzed by fear.

I was stunned. Even as two of his own employees were scheming behind his back to oust him from his own company, he couldn't summon the courage to do anything about it. He was worried about Mr. Kobayashi saving face, of all things. From my perspective, my father was showing loyalty to a man who'd actively listened to these takeover schemes and not bothered to tell my father.

I was incredulous—and *enraged*. I knew from that moment forward that my father wasn't cut out to be a CEO. He was a great man, a great scientist, but he would never have the backbone to fight when he had to. What disappointed me more than anything was that it wasn't just his job that was on the line. It was my job, my little sister Debbie's job—who had been working with us since 1987—and the jobs of many of our employees who'd also been with him since the beginning of SynPhar.

Begrudgingly, he allowed me to do what had to be done. I set everything up. I called the lawyers. I got things rolling.

Although I badly wanted to drop the hammer, my father had to do it. I give him credit for eventually mustering the courage. I was very proud of him for rolling up his sleeves and doing exactly what had to be done. He told the two rogue employees that a severance package would be on the table for exactly forty-eight hours. They could take the package and leave quietly. If they didn't, they would be fired, and one second after the deadline passed there would be no package. They both took the deal without hesitation.

Then, in a shocking turn of events, my father received a phone call from Mr. Nakagami informing us that Kobayashi was asking us to rehire the fired employees so that he could save face. I refused, even as my dad begged me to rehire them. He kept fretting about the dangers of losing Mr. Kobayashi's trust.

I stood my ground.

"Dad, we're not rehiring them," I said. "This is the Micetichs' last stand. A line must be drawn in the sand. It's us or them." In order to help him see the light, I turned his own argument against him. "Trust and honor? Where's the trust and honor shown to you?

If you hire these guys back, you're going to lose face with every single employee of SynPhar Laboratories," I said. "You've been empowered to run the company. So run it."

Eventually, my father agreed. We told Mr. Kobayashi we'd made our decision not to rehire them, which only compelled him to plead with us to hire them back anywhere, in any position. He didn't care if they were rehired as janitors.

But I stood my ground, pulling my dad along with me, who was somewhat reluctant, concerned, and very stressed.

What happened as a result? Mr. Kobayashi backed down. He broke off all communication with the two takeover plotters. He wasn't happy about what we did, but he understood it. And when rumors got out to the staff, they started looking at me differently.

It wasn't just gratitude they showed; it was respect. They'd recognized that I now understood the familial nature of the company, but also that I was willing to protect them. I'd bring out the big stick and swing it if I had to.

For the first time, I had my own leadership principles to lean on. You treat your employees like family, but you have to show zero tolerance for those unwilling to show you loyalty. Had my father been able to show some real toughness, I doubt a coup would have ever attempted in the first place.

If you're an entre-preneur, you have to make sure you create a business that has a positive, supportive, and trusting culture, but one that leaves no room for destructive politics.

If you're an entrepreneur, you have to make sure you create a business that has a positive, supportive, and trusting culture, but one that leaves no room for destructive politics. Make sure you have a zero-tolerance policy regarding the latter. You have to create a strong, highly structured hierarchy of leadership, which is something we were lacking at SynPhar.

For the first time in my professional career, my father and I got pushed—hard. He fell down, but I stood my ground. And when I helped him rise back to his feet, he was now willingly and gladly standing behind me instead of in front of me.

At that point, I thought I'd rescued SynPhar from its greatest challenge, not realizing that an even greater threat lay just around the corner.

CHAPTER FOUR

Wrestling My Inner Entrepreneur

Make no mistake about it. When you're an entrepreneur, one of the most dangerous traits that you or any member of your team can exhibit is naïveté. What you don't know and what you choose not to recognize can, in fact, destroy you.

It took the experience of watching my father's company nearly get stolen out from under him—via a duplicitous corporate pickpocketing scheme—for me to wake up to that reality.

Looking back, I realize we'd been woefully naïve. My father and I had willfully ignored the *real politic* truth that it's often the enemies within an organization that are the greatest threat to a company's survival.

Had I not put my foot down and forced my father to confront the takeover attempt head on and put Mr. Kobayashi on notice, both my father and I could have and would have been thrown out on the street.

I would have lost my job, and he would have lost the company he spent so much sweat, toil, and effort in building from the ground up. His life's work, stolen from him.

I can't emphasize enough just how enraged I felt in the wake of these transgressions. If you've ever found yourself betrayed in a similar manner, you understand what I was feeling. Anger can be all-consuming. I was burning, blistering mad. An inferno of resentment. And a "victim."

There's a somewhat unhealthy tendency in most of us to replay traumatic moments over and over again in our minds. We put them on a loop as a means of punishing ourselves for our mistakes, as if reliving the experience repeatedly will somehow lessen the pain or generate different outcomes. It also keeps us trapped in the past.

We'd been lucky. I'd intervened early enough to avert losing SynPhar, but just because we'd just barely limboed our way beneath the threshold for disaster didn't mean I didn't perseverate over every last detail of these events with teeth-gritting intensity.

I kept thinking the same thoughts, over and over. They were questions without answers, but that didn't matter. I had to keep asking them. *How dare they?* That was the frustrating refrain that emerged time and again.

How dare they take advantage of us like that? How dare they betray us after we treated them so well? How dare Mr. Kobayashi—my father's longtime business partner—even entertain such overtures?

The greatest thing about suffering through a professional setback like the one my father and I experienced is that it forces you to go inside yourself. It forces self-reflection.

I believe life is an inside game. We can talk ourselves into or out of just about anything, given enough time and effort. We can construct a fake narrative in our minds long enough that we begin to convince ourselves of an alternative reality that soothes our fragile egos. That's where naiveté can take you: down a never-ending rabbit hole of self-deception.

The better approach is to start focusing on the whys. Why did you think the way you did? Why did you act the way you did? Why did you remain naïve for so long? Why do you really feel the way you do about it? What part did you actually play to attract this into your life?

This path will lead you someplace very different—not down the rabbit hole to dark places, but to illumination. If you have the strength to keep traveling down this far more rugged path, you'll realize in the end that you have a great deal of control over how you perceive the world around you.

That's where naiveté can take you: down a never-ending rabbit hole of self-deception.

And in that realization comes true power.

Sometimes your self-perceptions can, in fact, become your internal reality. I know that's not an easy statement for some people to accept. You can't tell people that they can—and should—pull the good from the bad. It sounds too much like a New Age platitude. But in the world of business, as in life, we all have an ability to control how we view things. We can craft and shape the stories of what we experienced—what really happened—in either positive or negative ways.

You really can grab a pitcher of water, start pouring, and then declare either that the glass is half empty or that it is half full.

When the initial waves of anger and fire inside me abated, I realized that they had burned away some of my self-doubt. I'd felt confident and capable since the day I took the job, but it took the attempted takeover of SynPhar for me to actually start believing in myself. My own instincts. My own abilities. My own drive.

And once I started focusing on myself, outside parties ceased being a threat to me. The more time I spent drilling down and trying to figure out exactly what I wanted to do—and why I wanted to do it—the less power those around me ultimately wielded.

The point worth highlighting is that in many ways you do have control over your own destiny as an entrepreneur, especially if you start shaping your own future on your own terms—not on anyone else's. You can control your own intentions and you can control your own actions. You cannot control the intentions and actions of anyone else.

Somewhere in every successful entrepreneur's career, I think he or she comes to a similar realization. The variables may be different, but the end result is always the same.

So in the wake of the aborted takeover attempt, I stopped trying to appease other people. I adopted a new "no barnacles allowed" edict to my list of professional best practices. I held true to this new guiding principle in every situation—except, as we will see later, in one critical decision that haunts me to this day.

The truth is, when you're trying to do what you *think* is best for the universe at the risk of not doing what you *know* is right, you wind up betraying yourself, your company, and those you care most deeply about. The best course of action is to make a decision based on your life experiences, your wisdom, and your instincts and then go with it, full throttle. Make a decision, and make it be the right decision.

ONE DAY YOU'LL UNDERSTAND

In the midst of this metamorphosis, a strange thing happened to me. Making decisions became easier. *Much easier.* In the case of SynPhar, I realized that our relationship with Taiho had to be dramatically adjusted. Damage had been done; trust had been fractured. What my father and I really needed now was a new deal. It wasn't just the thwarted takeover attempt that convinced me of this truth; it was the increasingly incompatible differences between how I perceived SynPhar and the way our Japanese partners perceived SynPhar. My vision was of a glass half full; Taiho saw it as more than half empty.

> *The truth is, when you're trying to do what you think is best for the universe at the risk of not doing what you know is right, you wind up betraying yourself, your company, and those you care most deeply about.*

During the early stage of this relationship—what we'll call our honeymoon phase—our dealings with Taiho were relatively positive and productive. Although Taiho owned 80 percent of SynPhar, Mr. Kobayashi generously funded our research at levels that were agreed on with my father. But as the Japanese economy began to slide into what economists have aptly called Japan's "lost decade" from 1991 to 2000, the sanctity of that agreement became as thin as the paper it had been written on.

Given the economic malaise that drifted like some rogue cloud over the island and rained havoc on the Japanese economy for the next decade, it was almost inevitable that Taiho would feel the pain. In Japan, real estate and stock market bubbles popped, leading to a cascade of negative consequences, including lower consumer spending and nonexistent growth.

When Taiho's best-selling cancer drug, fluorouracil, came off patent and became available to the generic companies, the first thing company leaders did to offset this dip in revenue was to search for areas in the budget to reduce or cut entirely. Naturally, one of the first areas that all international companies consider reducing in difficult times is overseas spending.

When SynPhar was created, the initial understanding between my father and Taiho was that Taiho would provide funding to support fifty staff members regardless of the project. This was so we could recruit and retain a team of world-class scientists from around the globe. But the writing was on the wall that this was not going to last.

Across the Pacific, as the Asian economy suffered and their own sales revenue continued to drop, our friends at Taiho "let the tax tail wag the dog." Taiho concluded that it would be beneficial to them to run SynPhar at a deficit every year and write off the losses as a tax benefit in Japan.

It didn't matter that we had successfully brought in auxiliary revenue to SynPhar by securing research contracts with other pharmaceutical companies. Our net positive in SynPhar was viewed as a way to help *Taiho's* bottom line in Japan. We were forced to use all the revenues from our new contracts to offset the decline in Taiho's funding rather than to spur growth within SynPhar itself.

Taiho seemed committed to its tax strategy, so as SynPhar's deficit grew, so too did this point of contention. At the end of every fiscal year, we'd be forced to preorder—and prepurchase—all the equipment we might need the following year. Thus, we were being forced to buy things we didn't have the revenue to cover. This ensured that the color of the ink in our books remained red and Taiho got its tax breaks. As a 100 percent wholly owned subsidiary, this approach made perfect sense. However, as a joint venture company with my father as a partner, this was neither reasonable nor fair.

The environment and the economy were not the same as when the joint venture had been created. The personnel in Taiho who made all the initial agreements based on a handshake and honor also were not the same. As they retired, younger staff members replaced them and, in fairness, were forced to react in difficult economic times.

It was ironic, I suppose, that Taiho—with its ancient honor codes and obsession over saving face—wound up breaking our original contract, but as I mentioned, I was no longer naïve about the way the world worked.

This is a delicate way of saying that I was no longer going to run SynPhar the way my father had run it. I was no longer going to assume that years of dinner drinks, friendly phone calls, and "sacred" handshakes were going to entice Taiho to keep its word or, for that matter, look out for our best interests.

No one was going to "take care" of us. We had to take care of ourselves.

It was obvious to me that my father and I had to renegotiate SynPhar's contract with Taiho, so that became my singular goal: Renegotiate. Renegotiate. Renegotiate. After all, it was only fair that my father finally gained the security he so rightly deserved.

> *No one was going to "take care" of us. We had to take care of ourselves.*

A single phrase kept echoing in my mind: *Make a decision, and make it be the right decision.* Which was precisely the mantra I followed.

That phrase—which my family and coworkers have heard me say thousands of times—has become something of a personal mantra of mine. In my opinion, it's as simple as it is utilitarian: *Make a decision, and make it be the right decision.*

In other words, be decisive. If you're wishy-washy, you'll never get a buy-in from the people around you. On the other hand, if you're definitive in your tone and approach, people will follow you. They'll feel motivated, and they'll generally feel safe under your leadership.

You might wind up making the wrong decision, but if your choice turns out to be counterproductive, recognize that mistake and do what needs to be done to make it the right decision. Go full steam ahead—full tilt—and you'll make progress.

> *You might wind up making the wrong decision, but if your choice turns out to be counterproductive, recognize that mistake and do what needs to be done to make it the right decision.*

I've always believed honesty is the best policy when it comes to negotiations, so when I flew out to Japan to renegotiate our agreement, I cut to the chase.

Taiho and SynPhar had once forged a trusting and mutually beneficial relationship, but that was in the past. From our perspective, the trust had been broken, and our respective visions for the future were drifting further and further apart. What we needed was a divorce: quick, clean, easy, and mutually beneficial.

No marriage mediator, I insisted, was required. As far as I was concerned, there were really only three reasonable options available to both sides. Taiho could buy out my father's stake in Synphar. We could buy out Taiho's stake. Or we could wind down the company and part ways, coming back together over cocktails, decades hence, to rhapsodize about the good old days.

The only option, in my opinion, that was absolutely unaccept-able was maintaining the status quo, which would guarantee nothing but strife from here on out.

The response from Taiho's leadership was a flat-out denial. "No deal," they said. They were hell-bent on staying the course. They told us they'd continue to fund a single project at Synphar, our antifun-gal research, which required fifty scientists. After an additional year, Taiho's leadership would decide what to do with *their* company.

I told them that this was unacceptable, as SynPhar was a joint venture that was partially owned by my father. It was, in my opinion, a clear oppression of a minority shareholder. But I also knew the cost and difficulty of getting into a legal battle with Taiho.

My father and I were 100 percent invested in SynPhar, so Taiho had us over a barrel, in essence controlling our collective future. We didn't have leverage. If this was a poker game, we were all in. And Taiho was holding the better hand.

My general advice to entrepreneurs who find themselves in a majority-minority position is to do your due diligence early on. Come to grips with the fact that you're going to run into some kind of conflict with your partners. That is a given—a virtual certainty. So, ensure that you have a unanimous shareholder agreement (USA) in place, specifically one that takes into account all potential scenarios, and make sure your position is properly addressed in it.

It's exponentially easier to negotiate things at the get-go than to figure things out later. If you take one thing from this particular stretch of my story, it's that you must always, always, always draft a strong USA that assumes the worst. Negotiate hard at the beginning. Absorb that stress early on and it will pay off later. It's also in the best interest of all parties to do so.

What I learned from these frustrating negotiations with Taiho was that all good negotiators walk into a boardroom with a backup strategy. Today I know it to be a prerequisite for success. If you don't have a backup plan, you'll immediately find yourself in the weaker position. It's the business equivalent of entrenching yourself on the low ground while your opponents have staked a position on the bluffs, mountains, and high ground that surround you. You're beyond vulnerable.

The stronger the backup plan, the easier it is to come out on the other side of a tough negotiation. You have to devise that backup plan with as much detail, focus, and foresight as if it were your primary objective. You have to be so sure of your stopgap plan that you'll be willing to walk away from the negotiation table at any time without hesitation or regret.

If you formulate such a plan, I guarantee that you will sit in your chair differently. There's no need to reveal, in the midst of deliberations, that you have a backup plan in place. What's important is that *you* know you have it. You'll project a quiet confidence that will be palpable to the other side. The tone of your voice will sound more commanding and confident. Your nonverbal cues will project strength and assurance.

But that's only one half of the equation. I learned from my father that you have to show empathy and build trust as well. A negotiation is about people just as much as it is about the deal being discussed. It's about recognizing and appreciating what others bring to the table.

A negotiation is about people just as much as it is about the deal being discussed.

Empathy can therefore be a powerful tool. If you've done your homework and if, in the heat of debate, you can continually find a way to slip into the other party's shoes and understand what their "go" and "no go" sticking points are, then you're sure to make progress.

Couple that empathy with the confidence that comes with establishing a backup plan—one ready to be executed at a moment's notice—and you'll find yourself in a position of true strength.

After my unsuccessful attempt to sever our relationship with Taiho, I took my father's advice to heart. I didn't lose my cool. Instead, I tried to empathize.

Our counterparts at Taiho were not bad people. They were simply acting in their company's best interest. I realized that fear was probably driving their decisions. The implosion of the Japanese economy and the loss of the company's key patent were likely motivating them to take a defensive, "us-first" position.

At the same time, I also vowed that I would never again enter an intense bargaining session with Taiho from a position of vulnerability. There had been no stipulation in our agreement with Taiho that said I couldn't create an independent company, including one that could attract its own contracts.

New ideas began to flit to life in my mind. If I built my own company and attracted enough money from research contracts, I'd have a revenue stream completely independent of Taiho. My father could then approach Taiho and tell them he'd leave SynPhar to join my company if they don't compromise.

What we'd have is a real twenty-four karat bargaining chip.

There was really nothing preventing me from going off on my own except for the fear of failure. By this time, I'd accumulated enough experience to know my strengths and weaknesses. And for that, I have to partially thank a man named Paul Janssen.

If you asked me during my early years at SynPhar where I saw the company going in the decades to come, I would have wavered. Given the talent of our chemists, the options available to us were limitless. What kind of services did we want to offer? Did we want to chase new sectors, like genomics, or stay with what we knew?

For years, we kept our options open—that is, until I had a fateful meeting with one of the most influential scientists of the twentieth century: the late, great Paul Janssen. Over the course of his extraordinary life, Paul Janssen was granted more than a hundred patents, producing breakthroughs in the fields of mycology, infectious diseases, psychiatry, and gastrointestinal issues. As proof of his well-deserved lionization, consider that eleven of Janssen's medicines are currently part of the World Health Organization's Model List of Essential Medicines.[1]

I only met Dr. Janssen once in my life, when my family and I were spending time in Europe, but the details and impact of that single meeting are as vivid in my mind today as the first day I encountered them—proof that life-changing moments often come when you least expect them.

Dr. Janssen was an older man when I met him. He carried himself a bit like my father. Very distinguished. Gray hair. Well kept. With a seemingly limitless bank of knowledge about chemistry and business acumen to share.

My father, mother, and I were sharing dinner with Dr. Janssen at his family's house in Belgium. It was a simple affair. Once we sat down and my father and Dr. Janssen began conversing, it was off to the races. I listened and soaked up as much as I could, but my focus

---

1   "The Patients Are Waiting," Janssen Global Services, accessed 2018, http://www. janssen.com/patients-are-waiting-dr-paul-janssen.

was on trying to gain some insight as to which direction we should take our company.

Sometimes, I've found, it's best to be direct when you're sitting across from a brilliant man, so I asked Dr. Janssen, in the simplest terms possible, to tell me his secret. How had he discovered so many medicines in so little time, across so many areas?

In response, he just tapped his head. "This," he said, "is the secret."

"What do you mean by that?" I asked, a bit befuddled.

"Experience matters," he said. "In the end, everything comes back to good, sound medicinal chemistry." He rattled off all the pharmaceutical catchphrases of the hour. Genomics. Combinatorial chemistry. High-throughput screening.

"How many drugs have come out of any of those?" he asked. "Not very many. When you find a good chemist who's been with you a long time and who's worked on many different projects, that person is an extremely valuable commodity."

He went on to describe how, especially in North America, when a chemist turns sixty, most pharmaceutical companies put him or her out to pasture. Failing to value experience, he insisted, was a flat-out bad business practice.

"If you want results, you need to tap into one's experience," he said. "You need to respect them, learn from them, and bring people up who can learn from them. If you follow this and stay true to medicinal chemistry, you'll be successful."

I've never forgotten that moment. I was in my twenties. It was the late 1980s, but it's crystalized in my mind. I can still picture Dr. Janssen's home. I remember the mutual respect that Dr. Janssen and my father showed to each other. And the excitement I felt being in their presence.

But mostly I remember feeling the burden of trying to determine a future direction for SynPhar slip away, as if a big, heavy wool blanket was being tugged off my shoulders. Good chemistry plus good chemists can generate astounding medicinal breakthroughs. That was going to be the philosophy I'd hitch my wagon to moving forward.

I took Dr. Janssen's advice to heart. During my years as COO of SynPhar, with some great support, we'd taken a small fledgling company with four employees and transformed it into a highly profitable sixty-member operation by leveraging the power of good chemistry. Furthermore, I'd engendered trust with those scientists. I'd turned the lessons learned from Laura's passing into action.

If I set off to start my own company, many scientists would follow, because I'd made it known that they were needed—and respected.

We had a symbiotic relationship, and I'd told them as much—we needed each other to survive. I couldn't do the groundbreaking work that they were quietly doing in their labs every afternoon, and they didn't know how to commercialize that work into steady revenues.

So what was stopping me from launching my own company? Nothing but fear of failure. And yet I realized that I didn't really have anything to fear. We had already brought plenty of contracts and revenues into SynPhar, so I knew the business model was sound, and we had a team of scientists who could do the work. What was there to fear?

My father, however, still had trepidation over what Taiho might think and do. He saw the utility of my plan, especially how it provided him cover, but he fretted over the prospect of being sued as well as my ability to convince big pharma companies to sign contracts with an upstart company.

I knew at this point that I'd have to do this alone. As paradoxical as it sounds, I'd have to protect my father by temporarily leaving him.

First, I turned to the companies that I'd signed contracts with as COO of SynPhar. Would they be willing to follow, I asked them, and sign contracts with my new company?

To my relief, I found that I'd build up enough trust in my abilities to convince them to come with me, but I also needed the right scientists to oversee the research and deliver results.

In order to entice some of SynPhar's chemists to join me, I had to set an example, so I resigned from SynPhar. Those who wished to come with me would need to take a big risk and resign from SynPhar as well, giving up any benefits they may have accrued.

Because Taiho had no interest in SynPhar's third party contracts aside from the revenue they generated, and Taiho wished all of SynPhar's focus to be on an antifungal program, there were plenty of incentives for employees to do so. Due to the path Taiho was taking SynPhar, there weren't enough resources to fund research outside of the antifungal program. Employees could either risk being fired from SynPhar later (as their future in SynPhar was far from certain) or join me now in this new endeavor.

That was my one requirement: I wouldn't hire anyone from SynPhar unless they resigned and committed themselves to the new company.

My father, despite his reservations, was in agreement that this was the right move, so I took the leap.

In 1998, I launched DrisCorp Inc. I handled everything up and down the line. DrisCorp was my vision. I birthed it into existence. I was 100 percent owner. And I was proud of what I achieved, because I knew DrisCorp would help protect my father.

DrisCorp signed contracts with four companies. They were significant-sized collaborations, in which thirty-five chemists, hand selected, would take their initial compounds and make them more dynamic. They'd take compounds that had promise and make them even more promising.

And you know what? It worked. I knew I'd developed the backup strategy we needed—a strong safety net for my father and me. DrisCorp was a viable enough entity that I now knew that Taiho could never throw him out on the street. If times got bad, he could just come work with me.

During this time, my family, all of whom were on the SynPhar board, were expressing what would turn out to be a longstanding sense of entitlement—to the profits of the business, to the credit of mine and my father's work, and to the work SynPhar as a whole—while not being active in the business itself beyond me, my father, and my sister, Debbie. This developing tension amplified my creation of DrisCorp, and led me to begin searching through old letters and correspondences between my father and Taiho. Most of the letters were just regular business exchanges, but eventually I came upon a shocking discovery.

Right there in black and white in an early letter was a guarantee by Taiho stating that whenever my father wanted to retire, Taiho would be responsible for buying back his 20 percent of the company and paying him a retirement severance. He would then also be 100 percent free to go wherever he wanted, with no restrictions whatsoever on what he chose to do.

I couldn't believe what I was reading. The letter that I held in my hand was more than a bargaining chip. It was proof positive that Taiho would have to buy my father out.

Although I had left SynPhar to start up DrisCorp, I still felt a responsibility as my father's son to represent him in a fresh round of negotiations with Taiho. Given his lack of negotiation skills and his fear of conflict with Taiho, he needed me to be his advocate with the Japanese. So off I went back to Taiho.

I told Taiho's leadership that my mind had not changed. I still believed it was in the best interest of both sides that (a) Taiho buy out SynPhar, (b) SynPhar be allowed to buy out Taiho's share, or (c) SynPhar wind down and both parties go their separate ways.

Not unexpectedly, Mr. Kobayashi reiterated that his company's position had not changed since last year. I nodded my head, somewhat in disappointment, thanked the Taiho leadership team for their time, and went home. After much family discussion, which was needed to calm my father down, we all agreed that sending the retirement letter was the only way to go. I promptly emailed my dad's retirement notice to Mr. Nakagami, who forwarded it to Mr. Kobayashi.

The result was pure chaos in Japan. Initially, Mr. Kobayashi had many questions as to whether or not my father could actually take this action. Mr. Nakagami made it clear that it was indeed a legitimate agreement that Taiho had made with my father. He said it was binding, which is when all hell broke loose.

History has a way of repeating itself in the most fascinating of ways, doesn't it? Just as I'd fumed and questioned how we'd almost been the victim of a takeover attempt of SynPhar years earlier, now Taiho's leadership began to wonder how they got into this predicament. Why did they draft that document? Why did they sign it? How could they have made such a mistake?

The company's response eventually came via my good friend and mentor Mr. Nakagami, who laid out the company's position.

"We have agreed," Mr. Nakagami informed me, "that any time Dr. Micetich wants to retire, we will buy out his shares. We will pay him a severance package and he will be free to pursue whatever professional opportunities he desires."

This was followed by a direct response from the president of Taiho, who mentioned that he might have been a little hasty with his response earlier and requested an additional meeting. Company leaders backtracked like they were Michael Jackson doing the moonwalk.

"We should slow down," they said. Everyone had done and said things they'd regretted. Was it possible for this longstanding marriage to be saved, after all? The key question in my mind was this: Were they just concerned about winding down a company and how that might appear publicly? After all, we *had* built very good relations between Taiho and the university, as well as the government of Alberta. Regardless, the door was now fully opened for negotiations, and soon we had not one, but two great backup plans.

This time I knew I had the upper hand. My backup plan of choice, which I didn't share with the Japanese, was to invoke the terms of the contract, force a buyout at a good price, and then have my father come join me at DrisCorp.

Negotiations with Taiho labored on for a long time, until it became evident that the best win/win scenario involved winding down SynPhar and us going our separate ways. In the end, reasonable people made reasonable decisions.

The plan was simple: We would acquire the majority of assets from SynPhar—most of the intellectual property, equipment, staff, and liabilities—and they would keep the shell company, a few research projects, and the name SynPhar. They'd be able to continue a couple of the projects in Japan, and they could keep their accumulated research tax credits as well.

My father and I then immediately established a new company, NAEJA Pharmaceuticals, and rolled the assets from SynPhar into NAEJA.

I was quietly elated. There's nothing quite as satisfying in life as turning to your father, a man you respect so deeply, and being able to say, "Dad, we did it," and know that you played an indispensable role in that victory.

The only problem was that NAEJA was a 100 percent Micetich family-controlled company where siblings not active or familiar with the business were given board seats and voting shares. No one else was allowed in. And within my family the sense of entitlement and desire to control was becoming more and more insidious.

What was I to do, I asked myself, with DrisCorp? I knew what I had to do. I had to put a unanimous shareholder agreement (USA) in place in NAEJA. I needed to insulate myself, my business, and my dad's business against my family, who felt they deserved as much control and benefits as the two of us—and if not the two of us, certainly myself.

My father agreed with me that we needed a USA to avoid very obvious future issues, but when he tried to convince my mother, she rejected the idea out of hand. Although he was a great man, he always caved in the face of my mother's displeasure. He avoided conflict at any cost.

We'd have closed-door conversations, but it didn't matter. I'd lay out, in strictly logical terms, what would happen if we didn't draft a USA: My family could continue to reject all the work that I'd put into the business, all the knowledge and experience that I'd gained over the years. They would fail to see the risk that I'd assumed. The choices I'd made. The decisions I'd pushed.

They still didn't see DrisCorp as my creation; they saw it as my dad's work. Thus, they wanted DrisCorp to be rolled into NAEJA as well. And they wanted equal interests and equal votes.

I'd tell my father, far more presciently that I imagined, that I would be in for a lifetime of hell if we didn't draft a USA and, God forbid, something was to happen to him. In response, he'd placate me and tell me what I wanted to hear. He'd reiterate the fact that there would have been no NAEJA if it weren't for my vision and my actions. That it was my contributions, my courage, and my commitment that made all of this possible.

"I promise you," he told me, "that we'll put a shareholder agreement in place."

But, by this time, old memories and fears from childhood were beginning to well up in me again. *How could I keep my family intact? How could I avoid my mother's wrath? How could I make things right again?*

It was in the spirit of maintaining family harmony that I made the decision to roll DrisCorp into NAEJA without a USA. I felt that it was the wrong decision even as I was committing to it.

If I had made a stand and taken a similar approach with my family as I did with Taiho, it would have forced my father to step up and take a stronger position. He might have been forced to tell my family what needed to be done. But by simply going with the flow, I enabled my father's key weakness, when instead I could have forced a conflict early on and compelled him to face his own flaws.

But I didn't. I buckled, never realizing that it would be the most personally destructive decision I'd ever make in my life.

CHAPTER FIVE

No Ordinary Joe

It takes courage to be an entrepreneur. That may sound like a given—like an accepted truth that goes without saying—but the abiding importance of cultivating an aura of fearlessness in the face of uncertainty can't be underestimated.

I've never been convinced, for example, that entrepreneurs can be molded into existence. No business school in the world can provide the clay needed to reshape a risk-averse follower into a dynamic and driven leader. No mentor, regardless of their talent and passion, can chip, carve, and sculpt visionary entrepreneurs out of rigid blocks of prosaic-minded individuals.

Entrepreneurs cannot be manufactured or mass-produced. We're born, not made. But at the same time, I also believe that entrepreneurs require precisely the right circumstances for their talents to be actualized into existence. We all need support. We all need to push ourselves into situations that provide us opportunities to flourish.

And most important of all, we all require the pain of personal hardship to forge our true entrepreneurial selves.

My success in launching DrisCorp and NAEJA would not have materialized as swiftly as it did had it not been for the sense of honor and respect that my father had instilled in me. To this day, the way that I conduct myself in professional settings is a product of the values and work ethic that my father modeled for me for so many years. Reputations are built on actions, not words. If you abide by the old maxim, "Do as I say, not as I do," you'll never reach your full potential.

And yet I'm convinced that one of the major turning points in my professional life came years before, when I ordered what turned out to be a downright magical cup of coffee.

This was back in 1996, at a time when I felt my professional career was slipping into a veritable pit of quicksand. I'd just poured everything I had into trying to ensure the long-term viability of SynPhar, my father's company. And still we seemed to be on the verge of sinking deeper.

Our partners in Japan were reducing funding, tensions were coming to a rolling boil regarding my attempts to negotiate a new contract, and I was still seething from the attempted takeover of my father's company.

In short, I needed a drink.

On this particular morning, I decided that a cup of coffee would do just fine. So when I sauntered up to the counter of a small coffee kiosk on Granville Island in Vancouver, I pointed to a coffee cup and told the barista to pour me the strongest cup of joe she could muster. I'd never been much of a coffee drinker—I could take it or leave it. And truth be told, I didn't expect much of this particular cup of coffee; I simply had a desire to drink something—anything, really—

that could insulate me against the early-morning chill blowing eastward from the frosty heart of the Pacific Ocean.

As my coffee was being brewed, sending up wonderfully aromatic snake-shaped plumes of steam, my mind kept hopscotching from my concerns over SynPhar to the idea of opening up my own business. Now that I'd been blessed with children and my first wife had chosen to be a full-time stay-at-home mother, I felt that all-too-familiar pang of fear crater in my stomach.

"I've got to do better," I remember telling myself. "I've got to become a better provider for my family."

Sure, I was making decent money at SynPhar, but I still felt like a pawn on someone else's chessboard. SynPhar was 80 percent owned by the Japanese and 20 percent owned by my father. It was theirs, not mine.

I'd been thinking a great deal about Mr. Nakagami, my mentor and confidant at SynPhar. Back then, if you asked me to describe someone who projected the freewheeling, risk-taking entrepreneurial spirit I was interested in emulating, I would have pointed westward toward Mr. Nakagami.

Unlike many of his peers, he'd shown no hesitation in pursuing a variety of different ventures beyond his work at Taiho. He was an idea generator *par excellence*. Over the years, he'd explored everything from importing salmon from Vancouver for high-end Japanese hotels, to growing muskmelons for markets across the globe, to establishing a chopstick-manufacturing facility in British Columbia.

He was often viewed as an outsider in his own country. He simply perceived the world differently than most Japanese businessmen. He spoke English flawlessly and seemed to relish international business ventures. When he formed a strong opinion on a particular matter, he showed no interest in compromising on his convictions, even if his position ruffled feathers.

He'd regularly invite me to go golfing and talk to me about his projects and philosophies regarding business.

"Never tiptoe around the truth," he'd tell me, eyes focusing on the fairway before him. "Say what you want to say and be honest about your intentions, and people will respect you for it."

Then he'd arc his golf club toward his ball and send the ball soaring into the short grass in front of him.

> *"Never tiptoe around the truth," he'd tell me, eyes focusing on the fairway before him. "Say what you want to say and be honest about your intentions, and people will respect you for it."*

He saw something in me, perhaps shades of his younger self, even though we were from far different places and had been steeped in far different cultures. Unlike many of his colleagues in Japan, he never envisioned staying bound to a single business for his entire career. In Japan, when you start to reach your sixties, people start trying to push you out the door.

Mr. Nakagami was well aware of what was coming and wanted to walk out the door on his own terms, thank you very much. So it came as no surprise to me years later to learn that he'd left Taiho to join an international company building hospitals in Bulgaria. I admired Mr. Nakagami's pluck and derring-do. And now, having cordoned off some time to visit his home away from home in British Columbia, I'd begun to consider what outside business ventures might lay in my own future.

And that is the moment I curled my lips around the edge of my coffee cup and took a fateful slurp. I was shocked. When this particular sip of coffee rolled across my taste buds, it didn't taste like any cup of coffee I'd ever had.

I did a double take.

I smacked my lips, trying to preserve the flavor of the coffee on my tongue. Then I looked back at the coffee mug, tilting the cup ever so slightly so I could peek inside.

It didn't look any different than your typical cup of joe. Black as midnight. Steaming. A few rogue bubbles. Oh, but it smelled different. I dipped my nose inside as if I were taste-testing a fine merlot, and I could actually pick up richly distinctive notes, like coffee-crusted blackberries or blueberries. It was slightly fruity yet full bodied, bold, and rich.

I must have been quite a sight to the customers near me, as I continually dipped my nose into my coffee cup, slurped, and then purred with delight.

Eventually I turned to one of the baristas, still looking a bit starstruck, and asked her point-blank: "Why is this coffee so good?" If anything, she seemed to chuckle in response, as if she'd been asked that very same question a half-dozen times every day.

"We fresh roast our coffee," she said. "It's a difference maker."

She went on to explain how coffee loses 50 percent of its flavor and aroma two weeks from the date it's roasted—and that those same flavors and aromas degrade another 50 percent two hours after they're ground.

Immediately, a slideshow of images began snapping—*click-clack, click-clack, click-clack*—before my eyes. I pictured the interiors of coffee shops I'd visited over the years. Different countries, cities, states, provinces ... it didn't matter. You'd always see bins of neglected coffee sitting out in the open, exposed to the corrosive moisture-rich air and the destructive glare of direct sunlight. I had no idea coffee was a perishable product!

It was the equivalent of cracking open cans of Coca-Cola until they were flat as tap water and then selling them to the general public. Most Canadians didn't know any better. They'd been raised on a steady diet of stale coffee, so they just assumed that coffee had to be soft and bland.

But here I was, not much of a coffee devotee myself, salivating over every last sip. Imagine, I thought to myself, what real coffee lovers would pay for this stuff. Imagine how selective they would be if only they knew they had the fresh-roasted option.

As any entrepreneur will tell you, the thrill of a newly discovered business opportunity is the most blissful buzz on the planet. As soon as I took my last sip, my mind started percolating with ideas.

I immediately began investigating the cost and expense of roasting coffee beans as well as how I could educate consumers on the difference between good coffee and the lackluster stuff. The more I researched the market, the more excited I became.

I decided not to jump into operating a café right off the bat, as I realized it would take up too much time and too many resources. Rather, I began to see how, with a little help, I could get a coffee roasting company up and running while still fulfilling my duties at SynPhar. This was a great "backup" plan with a future I could influence.

I realized I *needed* to do this. Not for the coffee. Not for the profit. Not even for my family. But for me. This would be a test of my own making, one crafted *by me—for me*. Because ultimately, if life really is an inside game, you have to create internal challenges that you know deep down are going to be difficult to overcome. You need to stretch beyond your comfort zone, past all your self-imposed fears, insecurities, and self-sabotaging roadblocks, and well past the thoughts, fears, and insecurities of anyone else.

If you're successful running someone else's company, there comes a time when you have to find out if you can do the same on your own, building it brick by brick from the ground up. I needed to find a way to convince myself that I'd be okay no matter what happened with my father and SynPhar and Taiho. I needed to prove to myself that I could take my experience, vision, and talent and pour it, no pun intended, into something that was completely foreign to me.

If you're successful running someone else's company, there comes a time when you have to find out if you can do the same on your own, building it brick by brick from the ground up.

In doing so, I hoped to be able to look in the mirror and know that I'd laid the groundwork to one day break free of my family's control. Having worked in my father's company for so long, I wanted to get a little taste of what true independence felt like.

The next thing I did was go looking for the right business partner. When you're running a small business, this is one of the most important decisions you can make, second only to the idea itself.

I had a high school friend named Shane, whom I'd continued to play basketball with in a men's league in Edmonton. You can tell a lot about a person by the way they play basketball. Shane was the Canadian version of Dennis Rodman on the court. The guy was absolutely ferocious on the boards. He was also modest and unselfish. He looked to find the open man first and shoot the rock second.

He worked as hard off the court as he did on it. He ran a modest eaves trough business, but it was seasonal work, so I hired him to be our building manager at SynPhar. He was well liked and very ambitious, and the kind of guy who didn't mind rolling up his sleeves and getting a little dirty. He never viewed any job as beneath him. Shane saw the importance of every layer of work in an organization, and he excelled at every job he took.

So I sat down with him and laid out my plan. I was committed to renting some inexpensive second-floor space in Sherwood Park, near where I lived so that I could drop by on the way to and from work. We found the space, leased it, and then swiftly moved on to sourcing our beans.

As I'd begun to perform my due diligence on the project, I'd spent time researching our potential competition. I wanted to know who was as obsessed about quality as we were going to be. There weren't many, with the notable exception of a coffee roasting company out of Jasper, Alberta, named Rocky Mountain Roasters.

When building a business, many less-than-successful entrepreneurs make the fatal mistake of being too paranoid about their competition.

When building a business, many less-than-successful entrepreneurs make the fatal mistake of being too paranoid about their competition. They close themselves off from talking to others, especially those in their own industry. They keep things so secretive that they alienate potential allies, including experienced competitors who often are more interested in making friends than creating enemies.

It was Les Chorley, the founder of Rocky Mountain Roasters, who taught us not to make that mistake when we showed up at his door one day. We came bearing very little, except a sincere vision and more questions than a college freshman during orientation.

We told him, with absolute transparency, what we wanted to do: open up a coffee roasting facility that produced the freshest coffee beans in Canada. I told him why I was entering the business as well as my experience working in the pharmaceutical industry with SynPhar.

In giving a little of ourselves, we got a whole lot more than I ever expected.

Not only did Les share where he sourced his beans, he walked us through a comprehensive "do" and "don't" list as to what we should look for when we picked them out. It was an amazing gift, so much so that I asked him why on earth he was sharing all this valuable information with us so freely? After all, we were opening up a competitive business.

"For one thing," Les said, "I respect that you didn't hide your intentions, but you know what, Chris? When I was starting out, there were guys who helped me and guys who refused to talk to me. Today, I've got no problem going after the business from the guys who didn't talk to me, but the guys who did help me I'd never cross. In the end, the world is a small place, and I'd rather we be friends than enemies."

It was like something straight out of a TED Talk. Do good to others now, and they'll do good for you down the road. That was Les Chorley's golden rule. He could tell I was committed to this—that I was going to figure out, come hell or high water, where to source coffee beans and how to buy them, so refusing to cooperate would just create disgruntled competition he didn't need.

I've never forgotten what Les did for me. And later in life, I've tried to do the exact same thing, as partially evidenced by this book. Tell people your story. Offer others your advice on what to do and what not to do. Let them poach as much wisdom from you as they can, because in the end the act of sharing builds friendships that usually stand the test of time.

One of the single most valuable pieces of advice I can offer to young entrepreneurs is this: ask the questions. And one of the most rewarding suggestions I can make to experienced entrepreneurs is the opposite: offer the answers.

So as I began building my coffee-roasting business, which we named Windjammer Java Roasters Inc., I simply followed Les's advice. I flew out to the same coffee distributor in San Francisco that he used. Then I flew to Dietrich Roasters in Sandpoint, Idaho, where Les had bought his roasters and looked for some of my own equipment. And during my journey, I thought of Les every step of the way.

In the years that followed, my path and Les's path intersected a number of times. Never once did I go after business in an area where he was operating. When we did move into areas that I felt might be on his radar, I told him of my plans ahead of time and we talked it out. There were never any problems. The market was big enough for both of us—and then some.

There would be times, in the years after we first spoke, when Les's roaster broke down and he would call us up needing help. We were buying some of the same "green" beans from our shared purveyor in San Francisco and using the same make roaster, so we'd give him some of our coffee and allow him to sell it as his own, and vice versa.

But those "I've got your back" pleasantries came later. After Shane and I got our beans and roasting equipment in place, what we needed next was nothing short of brute-force strength. Both of us had agreed that we'd be the ones to heave our one hundred and fifty-pound bags of coffee beans onto our shoulders and carry them up to our second-floor space. Which is exactly what we did, one backbreaking step at a time.

If I've found one thing to be true about starting a small business, it's this: if you aren't willing to handle and oversee every aspect of its operation, at some point or another you're going to want to find a different business to get into.

Shane and I were willing to do all the work necessary to get Windjammer up and running, and yet it should be noted that hard work alone isn't sufficient to succeed. I learned from my father the importance of taking what I call the "me-too approach." My father never stopped studying. He read everything he could get his hands on, so

> *If you aren't willing to handle and oversee every aspect of its operation, at some point or another you're going to want to find a different business to get into.*

when some exciting news was published, he used to gather all the information he could about a subject and scrutinize every last syllable of it.

Then he'd call together his team of chemists and ask them to look over the findings themselves and determine if there was anything they could do better. Could they find some small error in the research? Was a better compound hiding somewhere among the data? Was there an overlooked tweak worth pursuing?

And almost inevitably there was *something* that could be slightly adjusted for the better.

That's the secret of how entrepreneurs can outmaneuver large, entrenched powers. We all adopt, in our own way, a "me-too approach." We know that given enough time and energy, we can make better products, boost efficiencies, and meet unmet demands in more targeted ways—if we stay nimble. The key is in moving your way around the roadblocks and bureaucratic barricades that often slow down big companies.

I often tell entrepreneurs to use their company's youth and lack of size to their advantage. That's how you compete with the giants: you find a way to give people what they actually need or want, as opposed to what they already have.

In the case of Windjammer, I was convinced that I was going to produce the freshest, best-tasting coffee in North America.

Remember my maxim: *Make a decision, and make it be the right decision.* It was time to put that philosophy to the test.

And how was I going to ensure that I had the best product available? By paying more attention to where and when my coffee was being sourced and roasted than any of my competitors. That was what would differentiate Windjammer Java Roasters from the pack.

I knew I couldn't copy anyone else's business model. I couldn't go out and do what others were doing. To this day, I recommend the same thing to every young entrepreneur I meet: go look at what everyone else is doing and try to determine what you can do differently.

The idea wasn't to chase big volumes in the early going. It was to convince people that they could experience better coffee by purchasing it from us. So instead of doing what almost everyone else does and mixing low-end, acrid-tasting robusta beans with the far smoother and velvetier arabica beans, we were going to sell only freshly roasted arabica beans.

Imagine every cliché you can muster about terrible vending machine coffee. We were going to be the rebuttal to those stereotypes. Not only were we going to focus on the arabicas, we were going to donate every single bag of beans or ground coffee that extended beyond its peak freshness.

There weren't going to be expiration dates on our products, but rather roasting dates. It was pure transparency. After two weeks on the shelves, however, any bags of coffee that were left over we donated to the local Mustard Seed Street Church, which sheltered and fed homeless people in the area.

We were unafraid to give away our coffee in the early going, because we knew we had a superior product. We also knew that giving away too much coffee was a clear indicator that we weren't running our business well. All we needed to do was to entice people to taste it, so I started running cupping seminars on the weekend, where I educated small groups on how coffee should be roasted, how it should be stored, and how it should be consumed.

I broke down the flavor and textural differences between coffee from Costa Rica and Africa. I offered taste tests. I taught seminars on how visitors could create their own coffee blends.

It took a lot of time for me to run these seminars, but they were worth it, because everyone walked away feeling far more knowledgeable than when they arrived. Before they left, almost everyone bought coffee on the way out, including extra bags for friends and family.

Those early days building Windjammer transported me back to my days at university. Sometimes we can get so busy with our daily lives and professional careers that we forget to take a moment to reappraise our past. My work teaching cupping classes—especially the personal enrichment I derived from sharing knowledge—reminded me why I'd gone into education and taken a teaching job at Colchester in the first place.

I began to wonder—had I strayed from that core aim? I may have been successfully running a major chemistry contract company, but had I lost a little of the independence that I'd fleetingly experienced during my first year out of university?

Truth be told, I simply didn't have enough time to weigh those difficult questions in the early days of Windjammer. Those days, we found ourselves giving away a lot of two-week-old coffee. There was a stretch of time when visitors to Mustard Seed Street Church likely consumed the best coffee they'd ever tasted in their life, completely free of charge.

But then word began to spread. And we observed how scores of people began driving very long distances just to buy our coffee. Our popularity was spreading like wildfire, to the point where we realized we needed to revisit the idea of opening up storefront retail space.

The one thing I didn't have was time, especially as I was beginning to launch DrisCorp and renegotiate my father's contract with Taiho. But we took the plunge anyway, feeling emboldened that the central foundation of our business was solid.

I purchased a ground-level business building unit on a busy street, which also had warehouse space, storage, and a back-bay door for deliveries. The new location remained in Sherwood Park, so I could continue to keep my commute times manageable, and soon thereafter we found ourselves with a permanent new home for our budding business.

We displayed our roaster in the front of the store so that people could see, up close and personal, the equipment we were working with. The cupping seminars were moved to the front as well, which continued to bring in droves of customers.

The only downside to this sudden uptick in activity is that I found myself struggling to find enough hours in the day to manage my responsibilities at DrisCorp while still overseeing the growth of Windjammer. Things were quickly escalating to the point where I needed to decide which endeavor I was going to commit myself to. Something had to give.

Then fate intervened, as it so often does. Shane came to me one day, eyes bloodshot, and told me that he and his Australian-born wife had been talking a lot in recent weeks. She desperately wanted to move back to Australia. They had two small children by this time, and she felt the need to raise them in her native home.

If you're an entrepreneur, you've no doubt found yourself in a similar pickle. You know you're going to lose invaluable employees during your career. That's a given, but when you're running a small business—in this case practically a two-person operation—losing half of your team is a virtual death knell.

Looking back, it was probably the best thing that could have happened to me, as this unexpected dilemma became a kind of personal final exam, a means for me to gauge the strength of my convictions. Ever since Laura passed away, I'd subscribed to the philosophy that coworkers should be viewed not as mere employees but as something closer to family members: stepbrothers and stepsisters in arms.

Now, as my business partner awaited a response from me that would, in essence, dictate the future of our company, I was forced to make a choice.

By this time, the calendar had flipped to 1999. I'd already created DrisCorp and was overseeing NAEJA. And, in spite of my best efforts, I was also struggling with my own family's ongoing entitlement issues and their more recent habit of not only downplaying but entirely disregarding my role in the success to date, chalking it all up to my father.

Who did I want to be?

Pledging allegiance to a personal creed is one thing. Actually remaining faithful to what you believe through actions and deeds is something altogether different. Do you learn from the harm inflicted on you by others and change yourself? Or do you soak up those strategies and project them onto others for your own benefit?

Who was going to win? That was the inside game being waged internally in that moment. Was I going to stay true to the business leader I'd become, or was I going to lean on the bitterness fomenting in my other business to justify a selfish response?

The answer, of course, is that I won the inside game. The new me.

I told Shane he'd never be able to leave when his kids started going to school. They'd become too attached, their roots would be set too deep. He had to go. Now, I told him, is the time to leave.

I didn't play any Taiho games. I bought back his equity, fair and square, because it was the right thing to do. And you know what? It felt good, even though my finances suffered. For a while I hired other managers to oversee Windjammer, but it was more of a stopgap decision than anything else.

I was too overwhelmed with all my responsibilities handling NAEJA to try to orchestrate an additional growth spurt. At this point, with three small children and a wife at home, I was going to the warehouse at one o'clock on weekday mornings to roast our coffee myself. I'd stay for a few hours working on various needs, go home and get a few hours of shut-eye, and then fly out the door to face my responsibilities at NAEJA.

A number of Windjammer managers came and went during that period. Some of them stole from the company—accounting audits proved as much. Sales weren't rung up, and money mysteriously disappeared, never to find its way into the cash registers.

I realized I simply didn't have the time to oversee Windjammer and NAEJA. But I couldn't bring myself to sell WindJammer Java Roasters. I'm sure you can understand why. It was *mine*, something I built with my own coffee-pocked shoulders and taxed brain cells. Windjammer had helped lift me out of a morass of self-pity and disappointment toward something approaching self-assurance.

Windjammer had proven that I was indeed an entrepreneur. So much experience had been distilled down and infused into this small three-year venture. I'd mentored and been mentored. I'd had a vision and turned it into a brick-and-mortar success story. I'd experienced good weeks and trying days. But I'd done what I set out to do.

"I'm ready now," I thought to myself. "There is no fear that can prevent me from trying."

So in early 2000 I began to wind down the coffee business. I

> *Windjammer had proven that I was indeed an entrepreneur.*

sold the assets but kept the name. The lessons had been learned—and absorbed. And as fate would have it, they turned out to be integral to what lay ahead.

To this day, my wife, Kelly, and my kids often tell me that I should have kept that business going, that it would have been a great family business for them to merge into as they graduated university.

I usually nod my head in silent agreement, never explicitly acknowledging that Windjammer is still up and running. It's alive and well—hovering there quietly in everything I've done since the day I closed its doors.

CHAPTER SIX

The Ties That Bind

What I remember most vividly of all is the shape of my father's tears. The way he'd avert his eyes from my glare as sad, gauzy bubbles began to form along the edges of his eyes. Like the man himself, they were delicate tears.

Some people can squint their tears away, squeezing them tight until they regress back to where they came from. Not my father. He had fragile tears. All it took was the slightest batting of an eyelash and they'd burst open, releasing sad, wet trails of moisture down his cheeks.

It didn't matter, at that point, how confident I was in my convictions. Forget about what was right and what had come before. Forget all those years spent at SynPhar, trying to shield him from bad contracts and disloyal partners. Never mind about the experience gained from launching my own contract-chemistry company or the confidence absorbed from brewing my coffee-roasting company into a respected business. All that peeled away, like an old stubborn hangnail, when I saw those tears.

After all, how can the cold, hard logic of a sound business decision possibly equal the emotional impact of a father's tears?

Sometimes I look back and wonder why I betrayed my own instincts, why I succumbed to my family's demands that I roll something that I'd worked so hard to build—DrisCorp—into a company that my family wanted greater control over.

And then I think about my father's eyes and all those confessions he wept to me behind closed doors. For someone like me who preaches the importance of pinpointing why we make the decisions that we do, the answer is fairly simple: I loved my father, and I wanted desperately to keep my family together.

It would be easy for me to revert to the old saw and say that if you do the right thing, you'll somehow be rewarded for it in the end. But that's the stuff fairy tales are made of. The truth of the matter is that sometimes you can do the right thing for the right reasons and generate heartbreaking results.

It might sound callous, but the more you can separate your emotions from the decisions you have to make regarding your business, the better off you'll be. The rule is: Compartmentalize. Compartmentalize. Compartmentalize.

It might sound callous, but the more you can separate your emotions from the decisions you have to make regarding your business, the better off you'll be.

Looking back, I realize that I should have dug my heels in—that all the frustration, anger, and tragedy that eventually followed was something close to unavoidable, especially given the individuals involved and the particularly thorny predicament we would soon find ourselves in.

I should have done what I knew was right and braced myself for the inevitable fallout, accepting the pain sooner rather than later. But I didn't, and I paid the price for it. Understand that you can control your own intentions and your own actions. If your intentions are honorable and your actions reflect them, stick to them with confidence. Never compromise them, and never feel you can control the intention and actions of others.

I'd built DrisCorp from my own vision, barreling forward with my father's support yet receiving nothing but criticism and defiance from my mother and siblings in return. It was a high-risk play, but I knew it would make my father bulletproof with a backup plan during his ongoing negotiations with Taiho. I'd built him an escape hatch that I could sneak him through in case of emergency. Then I used it as leverage to extract what was important out of his company, SynPhar, and transfer it into the newly formed NAEJA.

At that time, I was dumbfounded by my mother and siblings' lack of acknowledgment of my efforts. And frankly, I was hurt by their sense of entitlement. Both my intentions and my actions were twisted to suit a false narrative to the point where they even tried to insinuate I was trying to steal what was my father's all for myself, and then heavily criticized me based upon this false interpretation of my involvement. It was turning into a tug of war, and my father had become the rope.

On one side stood my mother, anchored by my siblings, who saw an opportunity to appease Mom and make some extra money as well. They were all pulling Dad in one direction. And there I was on the other side, unwilling to strain too forcefully to pull him in the other direction for fear of hurting the poor man and breaking up the family.

What my mother desired was equal shares for her children, regardless of who was working for and running the company. It didn't matter who formulated the plan, took all the risk, and brought it all to fruition.

As sad as it is for me to admit, these trials would teach me that sometimes *might* really does trump *intent*.

This much I believe. In life there's no such thing as equal shares. Some get what they deserve, some don't. Then again, my mother never claimed to be a realist. She'd built up ideas in her head as to how the world worked—or perhaps, more aptly, how it should work—and I pity the poor soul who tries to point out the warped logic undergirding those ideals.

In life there's no such thing as equal shares. Some get what they deserve, some don't.

If you're a young entrepreneur, you'll assuredly run into people like my mother along your journey. And if you're a seasoned business leader, you've likely already run into one of her doppelgangers. They are, for better or worse, intractable forces. Immovable as granite.

When my father pleaded with me for more time—for me to roll DrisCorp into NAEJA and then allow him to convince my mother to sign a unanimous shareholder agreement after the fact—I gave him the benefit of the doubt that he'd come through for me in the end. But in all honesty, deep down I was fairly certain it was never going to happen.

I have no doubt that my father went home some evenings with the intent of convincing my mother of her wrong interpretation of the facts—of the blind eye she turned to the role I'd played in SynPhar, DrisCorp, and NAEJA.

But I'm pretty sure I know what happened every time his car reached the driveway. Good intentions aside, he'd eventually find himself under siege in a barrage of alternative facts—you're foolish, Christopher is stealing what is yours, Christopher shouldn't get more than his siblings, Christopher can't be trusted—and then raise the white flag simply to slip out from under the fury of attack.

He made a critical mistake. He assumed that if he did what he needed to do and let my mother continue thinking what she needed to think, then everything would somehow turn out all right in the end.

My advice? Don't fall into the same trap. Nine times out of ten, when you offer undeserving parties even a hint of power, they'll do all they can to not only preserve their share of it but expand it.

Which is exactly what happened in regard to NAEJA. I caved on everything—all of my principles, all of the protections I knew were required—so that we could enjoy a temporary peace.

In that act of surrender, I suddenly felt like I was eight years old all over again. The old memories came flooding back. The finger-pointing. The protestations of innocence. The avoidance. The blame games. The lack of freedom and sense of self-determination.

> *Nine times out of ten, when you offer undeserving parties even a hint of power, they'll do all they can to not only preserve their share of it but expand it.*

Some of my greatest fears soon began to materialize. I'd hoped that going along with my family's wishes would compel them to come to their senses, but quite the opposite occurred. They claimed my sacrifice as a victory for themselves. Somehow getting what they wanted supported their self-serving narrative that I'd never done that much to begin with.

Rather than view my actions as a means to secure a temporary peace, a plea for family equanimity, they saw it as weakness, an opportunity to press for more. The narrative went something like this: *Chris didn't want to do this deal, but we forced him to do it anyway, so now we really have control over this company.*

This is what I regrettably refer to as the lion in the grass predicament. Whenever you give something out too freely, whether it's to your children, family, or employees, you're feeding a beast that will not be easily satiated. If the bonus, raise, or praise is warranted, then by all means show your appreciation. But if it's not deserved and you're merely trying to appease the needy around you, then you're committing a grave mistake.

You see it all the time in different aspects of life. The college professors who give out A's to C students in hopes of building their confidence. The parents who don't want their kids to feel the sting of loss or regret, so they shower them with everything their hearts desire. The bosses who give out well-meaning but counterproductive incentives to underperforming employees in hopes of improving their performance.

It never works, especially when it comes to running a business. Give the lion red meat free of charge and it will come to expect it. It will stop hunting for a while and begin to rely on your kindness. Take the meat away and resentment begins to fester. What was designed to be a perk inevitably begins to be viewed as a given. And sooner or later the lion turns on the kindhearted gift giver. In our family's Serengeti, the lions weren't used to eating grass—they expected gazelles.

This is especially true for entrepreneurs who choose to get into business relationships with friends and family. Never underestimate the deep and abiding damage that can come from nepotism. My advice is to tread carefully with friends and family.

Ask yourself, "*Will this individual I am thinking about hiring make an effort to perform better than my current employees?*" It is only in the assurance that they will pole-vault high above that threshold that hiring friends and family works out in the end. I know, because in all honesty I was a nepotism hire at SynPhar. The only reason I got the job was that my father ran the company.

Having been in that position, I know the unique challenges that such hires face. I wasn't accepted in the beginning. Most of my father's employees felt I was too young and inexperienced, and that I was granted too much responsibility.

They were jealous and perhaps had a right to be. I had people who tried to undermine me right out of the gate. And the only way I rose above that challenge was by shattering expectations. I performed duties that extended beyond my title, including regularly hopping onto Japan-bound flights to better understand and negotiate with our counterparts in Taiho.

In the wake of my decision to cede control of DrisCorp to NAEJA, I began to realize just how negative an impact that decision was going to have on the company's direction. My mother made it known to me that my little sister, Debbie, would immediately assume a prominent position in the company despite lacking the skills and experience for the job.

I fed the lion, even though it quickly became clear that my sister didn't have her heart or soul in the job. She saw it only as a paycheck—a paycheck she deserved by birthright—and treated it as such.

Although I loved and supported my sister, she saw all that I was doing at the company and knew I could see right through her, which prompted her to ally herself with my mother and my other siblings. She reported back to my family not so much what was happening but what would suit her the most in the end.

On the job, she demanded respect from her subordinates in an almost authoritarian manner. She didn't try to earn it; she claimed it as a necessary result of her position. And she was resented for it.

There was nothing I could do given the power struggles occurring within my family. If anything, the fact that my father suffered a stroke in 2001 shifted the focus away from these internal squabbles.

For years, my siblings and I had feared something like this might befall my father. Both my mother and father had always enjoyed eating and became increasingly overweight as the years slipped by. He'd tried everything from Weight Watchers and Jenny Craig to the diet fad du jour, but he never really committed to any of these programs. My siblings and I were united in our desire to help Mom and Dad get into workout programs and become more active, but in the end you can't force someone to do what they don't really want to do.

My father's first stroke occurred right before my sister, Brenda, who was two years younger than myself, was to get married in Los Angeles. Even though the stroke impaired the use of his right side for some time, my father was determined to walk Brenda down the aisle at her wedding.

I can still remember him, both at home and in the hospital, holding a spongy stress ball in his right hand and trying desperately to squeeze it. He worked on that ball for hours at a time. I remember those eyes of his, not blurred with tears but laser-focused on the ball. There was tenacity in those eyes. A fixated and purpose-driven obsession to will the nerves in his hands back to life.

He'd work himself into a sweat day after day, unable to even apply the lightest of pressure to the ball. He was relentless. He wouldn't give up. He was resolute and decisive, the complete opposite of how he'd dealt with Taiho.

And I could see in his vice-like focus how I'd inherited a great deal of my own drive. I knew that look. That was the look people used to tell me about back in high school when I played basketball. The look I used to give the folks at Taiho. The look I saw in the mirror as I was preparing to launch Windjammer.

I was part of him and he was part of me. Not in total, not in all aspects of our being, but in very important ways nonetheless. And even during those early, frustrating days, when the ball wouldn't squeeze, I knew he'd crush that ball in the curl of his fingers eventually. I just knew he would. I could feel it in my bones and in my blood.

And eventually he did squeeze that ball, his fingers twitching in tow.

But, unfortunately, the weakness in his leg never fully healed. And from that point on, he started looking old for the first time in his life, wrinkles and worry lines forming overnight.

Nevertheless, he met his goal. He did manage to walk my sister down the aisle at her wedding, a proud moment for all the members of our family.

By this time, however, I'd fallen into a kind of dispirited malaise at work. To add insult to injury, the entitlement issues welling up within my family were becoming increasingly counterproductive to the core strategies I was pursuing as vice president of NAEJA.

Revenues were still up, but the company was coasting along instead of soaring.

In 1999, we'd acquired all of the assets from SynPhar, including the contracts, equipment, and a little over fifty staff members, and rolled them into our new company NAEJA, which was followed shortly thereafter by the addition of the revenue-generating contracts from DrisCorp.

One of the first things I did, which I recommend that all entrepreneurs do when they find themselves in a similar situation, is to conduct a thorough housecleaning. The criteria for whom to keep and whom to let go are very basic. Ask yourself simple questions like, "Who do I trust?" and, "Who am I wary of?"

For years, I'd been observing how some of my father's employees had been reacting to our negotiations with Taiho. If you watch your employees, even on a cursory level, you have a pretty good idea who's with you and who's against you.

This might sound harsh, but if there is anyone whose loyalty is questionable, it's best in the long run to let them go right away.

We couldn't have people fomenting dissent by blathering on about the good old days with Taiho. Any efforts to undermine the new regime or the direction of the company was not going to be tolerated. It was a "no mercy" policy. If I had doubt or questions about a particular individual, their time at NAEJA was over. In all, this lead to a reduction in force from fifty-five employees to roughly forty.

If there's a shifting of the guard, and in this case the severing of a

> *This might sound harsh, but if there is anyone whose loyalty is questionable, it's best in the long run to let them go right away.*

long-held partnership, you have to make sure you make a complete break. If you're an entrepreneur, you have to ensure that you protect what you've helped create. I wanted to make sure there was no possible way for an employee to go around me and attempt a takeover of the company without me catching wind of it early on.

I'd already seen, while at Colchester Elementary, how negativity can eat right through the foundations of an organization. I was going to run NAEJA as if I'd been the principal of Colchester. I was going to do what I wished my principal had done and toss out the enemies within before they could do much damage.

After all, I had grand plans for NAEJA. By this time, my father had gladly adopted a backseat role in the company, even though my mother held firm to the fiction that my father was still doing everything.

It was a lie that my mother perpetuated in order to solidify her own position. If she, in essence, held sway over my father, and it was understood that my father was running the company, who ultimately had control?

These are the inside games that were playing out in her mind. Everybody knew her thinking. The staff knew it. Our clients knew it. Pretty much everybody we interacted with realized I was directing NAEJA. I'd embraced my inner entrepreneur, and my father was 100 percent comfortable—thankful even—that I'd done so.

After all, I had a vision for where to take the company. Just like with Windjammer, I wanted to ensure that NAEJA was moving in a direction that no one else had the guts to take. I wanted NAEJA to be a pioneer in the outsourcing of chemistry and biology research.

I'd come to this realization slowly but steadfastly. The wisdom offered to me by Paul Janssen had become imprinted in my mind as if pressed into hot wax: *experience matters.*

At SynPhar, we'd struck a deal with Taiho to take drugs from early stage research through to late animal-stage tests. We employed extremely skilled scientists who possessed the necessary chemistry and biology skills to make this goal a reality.

When SynPhar's relationship with Taiho had begun to fray, I created DrisCorp to offer these services to other pharmaceutical companies and found that they needed precisely similar help and were willing to pay good money for it. They needed good chemists and good biologists, which is exactly what we had.

This was a new practice within the industry. Years earlier, most pharmaceutical companies wanted to keep all stages of the drug development process in-house. They wanted to hire their own chemists and their own biologists. What they wanted was total control across the entire life cycle of the drug.

When the financial stability of the global pharmaceutical industry began to weaken in the 1990s, drug companies started looking for places to cut costs. Laying off basic chemists and biologists who handled the nuts-and-bolts early stages of development seemed like a good place to start.

Prior to NAEJA, there really weren't many contract research companies offering this kind of outsourced expertise. After years of cuts, the in-house talent of so many pharmaceutical companies had thinned. NAEJA, on the other hand, was extremely specialized and experienced in precisely what many of these drug companies sorely lacked.

There's no doubt that my father's name, not to mention his reputation in regard to creating tazobactam, acted as a major draw for potential clients. He'd delivered research that developed into well-respected medications. Over the years, my dad and his team had developed more than one hundred and twenty compositional matter patents. And thus we possessed an established, international reputation for being a trusted partner.

My goal for NAEJA was to leverage these dynamic strengths and convince large pharmaceutical companies to come to us to fill their research needs and to fine-tune promising new drug research.

You can, of course, see the irony of all this. This model freed us from having to enter into the kind of binding partnership that my father had been forced to create with Taiho. Embedded within this strategy was a degree of company control that my father and I had never enjoyed at SynPhar.

We no longer had to report to anyone else. We could pursue the contracts we felt were best suited for our company and our scientists. We were freer, professionally speaking, than at any time in our respective careers.

Yet personally, I was more shackled than ever. I'd put myself in a difficult position by not forcing the execution of a unanimous shareholder agreement. Thus, NAEJA's every move had to be approved by my mother and entitled family members.

I felt sick to my stomach about the whole affair. My siblings not only held a stake in the company, they had voting rights and board seats.

I actually told my father one day, "Dad, this is going to kill me eventually. We've got entitled family members who don't work in the business dictating what we should do. We have Mom's control issues. I can't get things done because it will lead to conflicts that will ultimately put you in the middle."

He said he understood, and he promised once again to try and convince Mom to sign a shareholder agreement. He knew that's what was needed for the company to truly take flight.

It never happened. My father was too busy enjoying the role he took on at NAEJA. He'd come in when he wanted to. He focused almost exclusively on the science. He let me handle the contracts and the conflicts, which took a great deal of weight off his shoulders.

I think he was truly content. And it was very rewarding to see my father enjoy his golden years. Revenues with NAEJA were steady. During good times, conflicts were easily avoided. My youngest sister was gainfully employed. My other siblings, who had their own careers or were supported by their spouses, would come to the occasional family board meeting to listen to my father and I give a status report on the health of the business. They'd offer their two cents, pick up their checks, and leave.

It was Dad who kept us together. But as any successful entrepreneur will tell you, what you should fear most of all when running a young business is complacency. Which is precisely what was beginning to take root at NAEJA.

> *What you should fear most of all when running a young business is complacency.*

I still did my job. The contracts still came in. The profits still rose. And yet I knew I wasn't in a position to take NAEJA to the next level.

The truth is that I knew we had an extremely dysfunctional and confrontational family board. Trying to get sustained momentum on any initiative of substance was next to impossible. Whenever I initiated discussions of new ideas, the eyes of my siblings almost immediately darted toward my mother and father.

Today, I advise entrepreneurs never to underestimate the benefits that come from having functional boards. The goal is simple: create a board with outside members who have a desire to add value to your company. Period. End stop.

It's all about value and vision. I've found that many entrepreneurs, depending on the level of control in the company, are rather fearful of organizing strong boards. Creating a sound corporate board can ensure strong governance strategies. It can bring in outside opinions as well as contacts that you wouldn't have possessed otherwise.

By all means, put conditions in place that will protect you. If a board member is creating problems, you have to have the ability to dismiss him or her and bring in somebody else. But don't make the mistake of assuming that organizing a board is an act of weakness, a signal that you're relinquishing control or setting the stage for someone to eventually swoop in and replace you.

A good board brings credibility to your organization. It doesn't matter if you're a small mom-and-pop business or a big international corporation. Take it from someone who's been thrust in the middle of a totally dysfunctional one: a functional board can generate enormous benefits.

Because my siblings weren't involved in the actual business, they viewed NAEJA as something akin to a dividend stock. As long as I was bringing in contracts and they were getting their cut, potential dustups were kept at arm's length.

⁂

Then it happened. On May 28, 2005, while visiting Los Angeles to see my sister Brenda and her newborn baby, my father walked out of his hotel toward his rental car parked outside the front door of the hotel. He tucked his head down to get into the car and fell headfirst onto the ground without even moving his hands to break his fall.

It was like he'd been struck by a blow dart. It was instantaneous. A crooking of the neck, a turn of the torso, and then the complete buckling of his body. From afar, the bellhops and bystanders assumed he'd slipped, but as they rushed to the car they realized he lay unconscious, immobile, and completely closed off from the world around him.

An ambulance was quickly called, and within minutes my father was sped off to a team of UCLA neurosurgeons. Phone calls were made to my siblings and me. At the time, I was in Kelowna in British Columbia. My brother was in Tennessee. One of my sisters was there in Los Angeles, while another was in Edmonton.

The message was the same for all of us. Dad had suffered a second and far more serious stroke. We were all to fly to Los Angeles as quickly as possible, as it was uncertain whether my father would survive the night.

That same evening, we all met in the waiting room at UCLA hospital. And soon we were pulled aside and informed as to what the doctors had discovered. My father had suffered a massive stroke, a huge bleed. He was on life support. Machines would be breathing for him for some time. There was no word on the extent of the damage, but the surgeons weren't sure if he was even going to make it through the night.

The roller-coaster ride began. The mornings and afternoons crawled along at a painfully slow pace while some of the nights were interminably long. Some days there seemed to be hope; others were filled with pure darkness. We had no idea as to the damage the stroke had done to his brain, but we were all there when the doctors informed us that his brain was swelling and that they'd need to relieve the pressure. Most of the time, we watched his vitals, bright green digital numbers, flicker up and down on the monitor. Blood pressure. Pulse ox. Heart rate.

My mother was a mess. As in any crisis, she just wanted to fight. She battled everyone who came bearing bad news. The nurses. The attending physicians. The surgeons. Her own family. Everyone and anyone who appeared to be an obstacle in the path that led to my father's survival.

At one point, my brother and I discussed that this might come down to us making *the* difficult decision. Eventually, we might need to decide to pull the plug. It was an uncomfortable conversation but an important one.

I'd spend a great deal of time with my father after his first stroke. I'd been there when he stared down at that stress ball of his and told me that it was the most frustrating, painful thing he'd ever experienced in his life.

"If I'm ever like this again," he told me, "you're going to have deal with it. I don't ever want to live in a state where my mind is disconnected from my body."

He knew that I'd been in hospital rooms like this before with Laura. The flashbacks were intense. The flurry of nurses. The beeping sounds of monitors echoing eerily down the halls. The blood stains. The facial expressions of worried family members pacing the waiting room. It was the most heartbreaking, soul-crushing fugue of déjà vu imaginable. In an instant, your universe changes.

I was convinced that if my father had been in any other city in the world, he would have died on May 28. It was his birthday, but it would have also been his last day on Earth had it not been for the UCLA neurosurgery team that stood ready and waiting nearby.

My brother and I discussed our options, but in the end we decided that the focus of our attention should be on our mother.

"Whatever Mom wants to do," we told each other, "we're going to support her."

I couldn't help but think how, even on the verge of death, it was my father who was bringing us all together once again. Once the bridge, always the bridge.

I couldn't help but think how, even on the verge of death, it was my father who was bringing us all together once again. Once the bridge, always the bridge.

We all gathered around his bed, watching him, talking about him, trying in some way to emulate and show his special brand of kindness to the nurses and doctors. He would have wanted that, we all thought, and if there was anyone deserving of us putting our differences aside to do the right thing, it was our father.

Then word came that my father had suffered a massive lung infection. I can still remember the nurse turning to us and telling us that these lung infections, if left untreated, typically kill patients, but that there was a miracle drug at their disposal called piptaz (piperacillin/tazobactam), which saves millions of lives every year.

That was the phrase she used: miracle drug. At which point I turned to the nurse and told her that the inventor of that "miracle drug" was the man lying on the bed in front of her. She smiled weakly—the kind of grin that projects both pity and disbelief—and began to return to her work.

"No," I said, "I'm telling you the truth. My father is the inventor of tazobactam. Google it. It's *his* drug." And so, she did. Likely she did so just to appease me, but then she found to her abject amazement that the unassuming man under her care had indeed founded the medication.

I remember my father's nurse holding the bag of piptaz in her hand for a moment and looking at it anew for the first time in years. Here was a pouch of liquid that had been hung on IV poles for countless patients in this hospital and in hospitals around the world for years. She wasn't exaggerating. It truly was a miracle drug.

My father had never used the drug for self-serving purposes. He'd never bragged about it or leveraged the influence of his creation. But he had been keenly aware of the good it had done, of the scores of people who were able to walk out of a hospital room just like this one because of his efforts.

And that, in his mind, was enough. During those long, painful days at the hospital, I began wondering whether one day I might contribute something of equal weight and importance to the world. Something that saved lives. Something that provided hope during moments of true darkness and despair.

The first thing the nurse did was stretch a piece of tape across my father's chart and print the title "Dr. Taz" on it. The next day, the staff photocopied articles about my father and the drugs he had created and taped them up across his hospital room. It was like a newsroom at the *New York Times*. Pictures. Text. Quotes. Stories. They lined the room. There wasn't enough space to tape them on the board, so they stuck them to his headboard and in different nooks and crannies of his room.

It became a kind of shrine, a tribute to a kind, unassuming man who had silently transformed the lives of so many patients both here and abroad.

Soon, he became a kind of celebrity in the hospital. Doctors and nurses came to his floor to see him. Surgeons unconnected with the case wanted to see the man who'd created tazobactam. It was a kind of awakening for me. It's one thing to see the revenues that came in from tazobactam and know that my father didn't earn much of anything, in terms of dollars, for his efforts. But I could see now that he'd earned something far more valuable—the acknowledgment of his peers. Better yet, all around us at that very moment, in that very hospital, you could stroll through the floors and see patients hooked up intravenously to his drug.

The impact of my father's work on the lives of so many people was mind-boggling in scope. He'd made his mark. Could I do the same?

> *The impact of my father's work on the lives of so many people was mind-boggling in scope. He'd made his mark. Could I do the same?*

Eventually, my father would emerge from his coma. We managed to get him home to Edmonton, but I realize now that he never truly came back.

At one point he could actually sit up in a wheelchair, which was a victory in itself. Sometimes his eyes would crack open, and eventually we decided to slip a book in front of them. We watched, to our amazement, as his eyes tracked the ink on the page. We were relieved—overjoyed even—until a doctor informed us that it was pure habit.

The connections between his eyes and his brain were frayed. We insisted that the doctor must be mistaken. We'd seen him make eye contact with us—and it appeared as though he could follow our words. He must be soaking up knowledge, we thought, just like he always did.

Plus, we'd occasionally see him move one of his hands up to his face to adjust his glasses, positioning them on his nose so he could keep reading, just like he always did. It was one of my father's signature idiosyncrasies. But when the doctor took the book and turned it upside down, we watched in horror as my father's eyes continued to track along as though nothing had changed.

It was at that point that I knew what was coming.

I received the call on November 28, 2005, when I was in Argentina. I was, ironically enough, speaking to a group of clinicians at the time, who were relaying one glorious story after another about tazobactam. Everywhere I went, I was showered with stories and handshakes and smiles.

Oh how I wish my father could have seen the admiration, heard the stories, felt the love from his peers—just one more time.

But when the call came to me, informing me that my father had died, I tucked my phone away, thanked my hosts for their time, and took the first taxi I could back to the airport. I was devastated. You can never fully prepare yourself for that call, no matter how inevitable.

It was the longest flight of my life.

I don't remember much from the funeral. I know that we made all the decisions together, one last time, as a family. My mom wanted the most flowers imaginable. We bought the nicest casket. We pretty much followed my mother's wishes all the way down the line.

There were morbid moments, like when we picked out a final resting place. It was a dual grave site with a big headstone. Empty space was reserved next to my father's grave for my mother, when her time came. It was hard for us kids, but it was therapeutic for my mother, which is all that really mattered.

Both my brother and I considered giving the eulogy, but we couldn't find the composure to say what really needed to be said. So I reached out to one of my father's oldest friends, Gerry Tertzakian. They'd experienced a falling out at some point regarding business matters, but in the end this professional rift never eroded the personal affection they held for each other as men.

Gerry was honored to give the eulogy and did a fine job. I listened, but I had too many thoughts of my own weighing on me to really take in his words.

When I saw my father's body for the final time, I kept looking at his face. His kindness was embedded in every fold and crevice. There were wrinkles in his skin formed from years of smiles and laughter, and crinkles around his eyes generated from years of reading and absorbing all he could from the annals of scientific medicine.

But mostly I remember his eyes. This time, they weren't glazed with tears; they weren't squinted into a studious glare or a look of fierce determination. They were closed now. Never to reopen.

I cried then—and still often cry when I think about him to this day.

My own tears have changed since my father left us. I cry my father's tears now. They are more fragile than they used to be. They dome around the edges of my eyes, frothy and wet. I don't hold them back anymore—I just release them, exactly as he did. They pop open easily, punctured by the pinprick of a thousand memories of a good man who taught me, through his own words and actions, the true definition of "heroism."

CHAPTER SEVEN

Throwing Our Hat
Into the Ring

When I returned to work following my father's passing, I marched into NAEJA's offices with the same determination I showed in years past. I got there early before anyone arrived and hustled my way across the floor like a determined marathoner on his way past mile marker one. I was ready to pack in a full day's work.

I parked in my usual parking space, went through front door past reception, down the hallway, to my office, then back down the hall and up the stairs, and finally to my ultimate destination, just past the administration lunchroom: a closed door on the right at the end of a hall on the second floor.

That's when my pace slowed, and as my hand cupped around the doorknob, it froze in place.

If you're an entrepreneur, you know a thing or two about closed doors—both the physical and metaphorical variety. But this door was different. On the other side of this door lay both opportunity and pain.

My father's voice would never fill that room again. In his wake would just be silence and loss.

I suppose I could have directed someone else to go in and clean up my father's office for me. All of his things could have been slipped neatly into boxes for me to look through when my emotions were less raw. Desks could have been swapped, bookshelves restocked. I could have tried to gloss over the emotions hiding in that room with some primer and a new coat of paint. But in the end, does delaying the ache ever really dull the pain?

An old refrain kept humming in my ears: *Do the things that you don't like doing, Chris.*

I don't think I've ever felt as alone as I did that morning. By this time, the differences between my wife and I had become irreconcilable, which would soon lead to the dissolution of our marriage. With the passing of my father, there was no longer anyone in my family who supported my vision for NAEJA, perhaps with the exception, I assumed at the time, of my little sister Debbie and a few loyal souls. And here I was about to walk into my father's office, sit in his chair, and officially become the CEO and president of our company.

I'd been the de facto head of NAEJA since we parted with Taiho, but I knew that sliding into my father's chair would mark a new chapter in my life.

"I'm on my own now," I thought to myself, feeling a pang of loneliness punch me in the solar plexus.

And still, that voice: *Do the things that you don't like doing, Chris.*

What's interesting is that I can still see all the objects lining my father's desk. His books. Picture frames. And all those decorative masks he collected from around the globe—enough of them to represent each country of the United Nations. But it's the image of my father's personal assistant, Caroline Kong, that snaps most sharply into focus with me now.

Caroline was as fiercely protective of my father like those glorious old film noir secretaries who took care of Humphrey Bogart back in the 1940s. Caroline was my father's right hand—his fingers and all. He'd dictate notes and memos and she'd translate them into letters and emails. She was the one who reminded my father when it was time to send another bouquet of fresh flowers to my mother. And the one who'd pick up the phone and persuade—*demand* might be a better word—that a certain CEO or chief scientific officer sit down for a meeting with Dr. Micetich. Most of those poor souls didn't know what hit 'em. Surely they hung up the phone wherever they were—Japan, New York, Edmonton—and muttered to themselves, "What just happened?"

Around the office, we had a nickname for Caroline Kong: The Great Wall of Caroline. She was Chinese, thus the geographic reference, but mostly it was a sobriquet borne from the fact that she didn't allow anyone—and I do mean *anyone*—to slip past her desk (i.e., Caroline's checkpoint) to see my father if they didn't have an appointment.

Although Caroline's protective nature could be frustrating at times for the rest of us, she became a beloved member of the NAEJA team.

It took a few months for Caroline and I to get on the same page. I didn't need—or want—her to put my every thought to paper. I could write my own emails, thank you, but there was something in the way she treated me in those initial days after my father's passing that gave me both comfort and consolation.

Caroline was old school. Harsh. Honest. Honorable. The way she saw it, executive secretaries weren't paid to judge or voice their approval or disapproval. But I saw the love, and my employees saw it. In treating me exactly the way she treated my father, Caroline said all she needed to say without ever saying a word.

After all, if Caroline is with you, who can be against you?

Helping to shepherd an organization through the loss of a beloved figurehead can be very challenging indeed. If you're an entrepreneur and tragedy strikes—whatever that tragedy may be—you have to be willing to put on a cheerful mask. Become, if you must, a corporate Janus: a god of two faces.

If you're an entrepreneur and tragedy strikes—whatever that tragedy may be—you have to be willing to put on a cheerful mask.

Grieve in your own way on your own time, but make sure you boost the confidence of your employees and reassure them that the fate of the company—and their jobs—is in good hands.

My advice to business leaders who've experienced a loss or found themselves in a negative rut is to find a way to give your employees a place to vent. Create forums where their emotions can pour forth, opportunities for them to weep or remember or voice their concerns, but also give them something to be confident about. Don't let stasis set in, which can ice over and develop into a paralyzed work force.

In my particular situation, things were certainly not all roses and rainbows inside NAEJA's boardroom, but I kept my frustrations to myself.

The negative repercussions of my mother's unwillingness to sign the unanimous shareholder agreement immediately reemerged, especially in regard to a life insurance policy I set up for my father through NAEJA.

The origins of this particular blowup extended back to the origins of NAEJA, when I insisted that individual life insurance policies be purchased for all the shareholders of the company, including my father.

In the unsigned shareholder agreement, I had stipulated that any moneys paid out from these policies should be directed back to NAEJA to reacquire the deceased's shares in the company. I didn't play favorites. Had I passed away, my life insurance policy would have been cashed out to buy out my shares as well. And the same was true for my mother and siblings.

This is a standard clause in any shareholder agreement, designed to prevent those not working in the business and those not intimately familiar with the business from suddenly becoming active partners due to a death.

Although NAEJA had been paying the premiums for these policies, my mother balked at the suggestion that the company owned the policy. As far as my mother was concerned, she owned the policy and should receive the payout as well as retain all of my father's shares.

In an instant, the old fears and desire to avoid my mother's wrath reemerged. I was alone in my dissent. My siblings knew that by propping up my mom's position they were protecting their own.

Things got a bit testy in our discussions, eroding away whatever temporary unity we'd forged during my father's health struggles. In the end, entitlement trumped the long-term best interests of the company. Mom received her money and her shares, and I did my best to focus my energies elsewhere.

Personally, I feel that hardships can be an entrepreneur's best friend. They motivate us. They propel us to take on new challenges. For me, the mere act of staying busy is the ultimate antidote to hard times.

> *Personally, I feel that hardships can be an entrepreneur's best friend. They motivate us. They propel us to take on new challenges.*

So I threw myself into my work. Fortunately, I'd already established a blueprint for success. I'd steered NAEJA into a position where the natural tailwinds of our contract work were propelling us forward. Even in the face of resistance and doubt from my family, NAEJA expanded. The economy was humming along, so we were able to get more aggressive in acquiring contracts and hiring more scientists.

After my father's passing, from 2005 to 2008, we grew the company from sixty-five to one hundred and thirty employees. Revenues steadily increased, which curbed whatever criticisms my mother and siblings might have wanted to level at me. And yet my mother still found it difficult to stay silent.

At occasional board meetings and public functions with staff, it became increasingly common to hear my mother talk about how well "her" company was doing.

Her words began to eat away at me, one caustic syllable at a time. After a while, they became almost too corrosive to bear, as my mother shifted from merely downplaying my role in NAEJA's success toward giving credit for all the company's growth and accomplishments to my deceased father.

This isn't a rare phenomenon. When times are good, everyone wants to sit at the head of the table. But what I knew—and what far too many entrepreneurs fail to realize—is that finding a niche in your industry yields only momentary relief. You have a small window of opportunity to make a profit. Then, you've got to evolve if you want to survive. Try holding onto that niche for too long, and competitors begin wrestling away market share, your company quickly devolves into shark bait.

Looking back, I should have pumped as much of our revenues back into NAEJA as possible, building up a large enough reserve to insulate the company from future threats. There's little doubt in my mind that my family—who lined up for their NAEJA dividend checks like children on Christmas morning—would have blocked my efforts, but in the end I'll never truly know, because I never pressed the subject.

Nevertheless, the effects of witnessing my father's drug tazobactam save his life had a profound effect on me. My father and I had always believed in pursuing underground research on promising new compounds. Under my leadership, I doubled down on those efforts.

Why now? Because I could see the broad outlines of real danger on the horizon, as foreign competitors began to muscle into our research niche. Should competition for our services become too cutthroat, NAEJA had the potential to collapse in on itself with all the speed and suck of a Florida sinkhole.

From 2005 to 2008, companies in India and China began to dramatically undercut rates offered by North American companies like our own, weakening the foundation of NAEJA's largest source of revenue.

As an entrepreneur, it's essential to invest in differentiators before they become necessary. And you have to allocate the necessary resources to those patents, products, or services while you're growing—not after the downturn, when you absolutely need them. Finding that extra something—the honey in the tea, so to speak—will make you stand out from the crowd when dark days arrive.

> *As an entrepreneur, it's essential to invest in differentiators before they become necessary.*

I knew that NAEJA's drug discovery expertise was our key differentiator. So I leveraged that strength when competition ramped up. When we met with a client, we didn't just showcase our chemistry and biology services, we also looked into what kinds of compounds our clients might be researching internally. If we had something in our own research pipeline that matched their interests, we'd offer them the opportunity to acquire our research in exchange for contracted back work.

Although our research had the potential to deliver plenty of drugs to others on a fee-for-service basis, I knew from inception that when we came across something truly groundbreaking we had to hold onto it and advance it as far as possible, as opposed to giving it away early. The contract research business was fast drying up, and NAEJA's business model coupled with our family conflicts and the lack of a large reserve fund made advancing any of our own internal programs within NAEJA virtually impossible.

In the immediate years leading up to the global financial crisis, we achieved a kind of complacent stasis. We rode the waves and focused on the pleasures of the present as opposed to the dangers of the future. My birth family was, in the very least, holding together, although bound by a delicate and fraying web of self-interest.

And then came the financial earthquake that was 2008. As chaos rippled through the capital markets, its aftershocks radiated out in all directions, generating abject chaos in the pharmaceutical industry. NAEJA took its licks, losing some major contracts—including one that affected twenty-three of our employees—as big pharma turned to dirt-cheap research partnerships overseas.

For some time, we had targeted small- and medium-sized companies that didn't have the time or patience to deal with India or China, especially those that could benefit from the speed and efficiencies we could generate. Post 2008, that strategy was accelerated, but it was simply a stopgap—a means to a different end.

More than once I found our budgets stretched to the limit. Some say that you're not a "true entrepreneur" unless you've been forced to juggle your way to meeting your payroll. Over my career, I can safely say that I have more experience juggling than a clown in a circus act.

In 2008, I didn't know how I was going to manage payroll for the week at hand let alone three or four months in the future. Pressure mounted from my two siblings who weren't working in the business, Keith and Brenda. When times were great, they never once said, "Well done." But, when times were tough, they were very quick to offer harsh criticism.

"You don't travel enough," they told me. Or, "You travel too much. You have no sales experience. We can't afford to hire sales specialists."

It was Kafka-esque—an absurd nightmare, which I tried to overcome by stressing that NAEJA needed to evolve to meet the needs of a rapidly changing economy.

Whenever I counsel entrepreneurs about the dangers of sudden downturns, the first thing I tell them is that downturns are, by nature, unpredictable. And yet you can insulate yourself from much of the damage by formulating a plan and sticking to it. Remember the Micetich maxim: *Make a decision, and make it be the right decision.*

> *Whenever I counsel entrepreneurs about the dangers of sudden downturns, the first thing I tell them is that downturns are, by nature, unpredictable.*

In NAEJA's case, that meant continuing to develop our own discovery program. When contracts started disappearing, I directed my right-hand man and NAEJA's vice president of business development, Sameeh Salama, to focus our efforts on researching a new beta-lactamase inhibitor, a kind of "next-generation" tazobactam.

I saw opportunity in the anti-infective arena. If tazobactam had long been a drug of first choice in hospitals across the world, how much longer could it stay ahead of the virulent superbugs that were rendering so many antibiotics ineffective?

I would be remiss if I didn't admit that personal reasons also played a role in my decision. Wouldn't it be amazing, I thought, if I could stand on my father's shoulders and create a drug that had the same impact on my generation that my dad's drug did on his? Could there be any more rewarding way to honor my father's legacy, while also making my own mark at the same time? If I could develop that follow-up drug and license it to a large pharmaceutical company, I could save NAEJA.

Thus, in 2010 when our chemists synthesized a very difficult to make reference compound that was in clinical trials, under the guidance of Dr. Samarendra Maiti, I had them "play around" with the molecule to see if we could pound our own intellectual stake into the ground.

Dr. Maiti is a brilliant chemist, short in stature and enormous in personality. "Maiti," as we call him (perhaps a more appropriate moniker would be "mighty"), had worked for my father prior to the formation of SynPhar, and is one of the inventors named on the tazo-bactam patent. Earlier, Paul Janssen told me that the key to success was to find great people with experience, respect their worth, and keep them. Dr. Maiti, who had initially been my father's chemistry guru, soon became mine, and he has led my teams of scientists for over thirty years.

In short order, my chemists started bringing back data for a compound that seemed capable of eclipsing some of the other anti-infectives being researched. Although it was too early to get too excited about the findings, I realized I had to go all in to see the research to fruition. Considering the rapidly declining contract research organization (CRO) industry for North American companies, we did not have the luxury of time.

My family saw things differently. They were skeptical of my plans and wanted to stay the course, so in a last-ditch effort, we reduced our rates in NAEJA to ridiculous, barely break-even levels. And still we couldn't attract enough research contracts. By this time, criticism from my siblings had reached an apex. They attacked every aspect of the business without presenting any viable ideas as to how they would right the ship. Inside the NAEJA boardroom, it was full-out war between my siblings and me.

It was childish, really. Lots of yelling. I was given plenty of advice on how to do things the "right" way, but when I spoke everyone pretty much plugged their ears and droned out my ideas. Between the business stress and their criticism—which in hindsight had very little to do with the actual business—we were all to blame for the destruction of our family. Without a solid unanimous shareholder agreement in place, business issues could not be separated rationally from our personal issues. My little sister Debbie and I were all in with NAEJA; the others were not.

Ah, but there was someone listening. One special person, whom I had met more than a half a decade earlier.

Have you ever been fortunate enough to meet someone who makes such an everlasting impression on you—an actual physical and emotional imprint on your soul—that they haunt your thoughts and dreams from that day forward?

You meet. You hit it off. And you feel in that moment that there's something indestructible about the bond that's been forged between you. Maybe the circumstances don't allow you to find each other in that moment, but you willfully let the sweet memory of that first encounter haunt you everywhere you go.

You have a good day and you role-play in your mind what it would feel like if you could share the news with them. You imagine what words might be exchanged. You try to picture the curl of their smile. The shine in their eyes. The arch of their eyebrows in the wake of an unexpected surprise.

I was haunted by Kelly Alexandra Leganchuk since we first met, on September 22, 2001. I hadn't given up on my marriage at that time, but it was already splintering apart. That night I had gone to an Edmonton Oilers game with my friends, who then dragged me out to a local nightclub called Overtime to extend the evening with a few cocktails.

When I saw Kelly walk in the door—with her beautiful blonde hair and her body swathed in a black winter coat—my eyes peeled sharply in her direction. She had an aura of fearlessness about her that was irresistible.

My friends, embroiled in a chauvinistic debate as to who qualified as the most beautiful woman in the room, asked for my opinion. I didn't hesitate. "That woman," I said, motioning toward Kelly.

Big mistake. With friends like mine, who needs enemies? Intent on trying to see who could make me blush the deepest shade of princess pink, one of my friends, unbeknownst to me, walked over to Kelly and informed her that I was interested in a dance.

Upon returning, my unwanted wingman informed me of the dilemma I now faced: embarrass myself by going over, or humiliate myself by not going over. I did the chivalrous thing. I told Kelly—who was, by the way, also the most charming woman in the place—that there were forces beyond our control encouraging us to dance. Would she be interested in joining me on the dance floor?

She said she'd just ordered a drink and needed time to warm up. So I returned to my friends, who relished what they perceived to be Kelly's rejection of me. While my friends made fun, Kelly kept watching me and walked over to save me. She reached through them, grabbed my hand, and guided me onto the dance floor.

I don't, for the record, dance. But for Kelly, I did. We danced. We talked. We laughed. And eventually we went our separate ways after we left the club.

Two days later, I found her phone number, called her and confessed that I was in fact married but that I needed to meet her for coffee to explain. Initially she hesitated. But since I knew she was a travel agent, I said it was either coffee or I'd drive to her office and book a trip to some faraway land—Afghanistan sounded nice that time of year—so that we'd have to spend an hour planning things out.

Over coffee we agreed that we'd met at the wrong time. I knew precisely where my marriage was headed, but I had a responsibility to see it through. I felt that explaining my situation to Kelly in person was more honorable than simply never contacting her again and leaving her guessing as to why.

We both moved on. Eventually, my marriage ended of its own accord and one of Kelly's relationships led to two children. With all my work and my responsibilities to my own children, who were my world, I was fine being single. Eventually, Kelly watched as her own relationship ended.

We'd casually kept in contact with each other since 2001, but these weren't the kind of calls you'd make to a friend. They were deeper. When my father passed away in 2005, it was Kelly Alexandra whom I wanted to pour out my heart to. And later I learned that she had similar feelings herself.

Her first child. Career success. A new paint scheme in her house. She'd often think to herself, "I wonder what Chris would say about all this?"

It was in 2008, when Kelly's own relationship came to a close, that we started really talking again. Seven years of hypotheticals— What would Kelly think about this? What would Kelly think about that?—turned into real words and real smiles and real laughter.

The truth is that I'd closed the door on the possibility of finding true love a while before, and I'd kept that door closed for a long time. In fact, I'd padlocked it. Added deadbolts. Pulled the handle to make sure it was sealed tight. Because there was only one woman I wanted to find waiting on the other side, and that was Kelly.

In 2008, when I realized she was now there waiting patiently behind that door, I couldn't undo those locks fast enough. The locks clinked and slid away as if Houdini himself were unbolting them.

For the first time since my father's passing—or perhaps for the first time in my entire life—I was no longer truly alone. I had my love and my champion.

It was through my relationship with Kelly that I began to develop a clearer understanding of what love and support should look and feel like. I had a frame of reference now. Kelly's support came without conditions. She listened, processed, and then advised. No subterfuge. No guile. No selfish ulterior motives.

It was through my relationship with Kelly that I began to develop a clearer understanding of what love and support should look and feel like.

Did we—and do we still—get into arguments? Absolutely. But in truth, we grapple more than fight. We wrestle with each other's ideas and perspectives, not to pin each other down and win the debate but to collectively shape our individual opinions into something better and stronger.

If you're able to build trust and a connection with someone, you'll find that you demand more of yourself in the process. Kelly gave me something that I'd never been able to rely on from my own flesh and blood—the assurance that someone would stand by me during trying times and patiently help me overcome my shortcomings.

Things I had once accepted as givens with my family suddenly looked and felt deeply flawed. You assume that your family should be a constant force for good in your life, but what if their actions wind up having the opposite effect?

Maybe the first step toward independence—both personally and professionally—is defiance: the willful decision not to allow the self-destructive behavior of others to get in the way of what you believe in.

Perhaps the only way for me to find myself—and *prove* something to myself—was to pursue the follow-up to tazobactam and run with it. And to hell with the fallout.

I remember making a ten-hour drive back from one of Kelly's family gatherings in Manitoba. We'd been golfing all day. Lots of men and women in funny hats. Golf balls flying everywhere. A couple of pull-your-hair-out missed putts on the green.

I'd been talking all day about my troubles with NAEJA and my family, which had begun to wear on me. I remember turning to Kelly on the way home and saying, "Talk. Talk. Talk. I'm tired of talking about NAEJA. It's going nowhere. I need to start doing something about it."

At which point Kelly turned to me and said, "What's the first thing you need to breathe life into your ideas? What do you need to get started?"

I said, "Well, we need a company name. No one is going to invest in something dubbed New Co. Inc. We need a name. Something people can buy into."

It's true. Never underestimate the importance of a company name. When you see a name or hear a name, you want it to stand for something. Make it memorable. Make it symbolic. But don't assume that you have to come up with one that's linked to your given industry. Think more about the invisible feelings and emotions that well up in someone who hears that name. Can you build a memorable logo around it? Can you market that name in a way that makes it stand out from its competitors? Is it short, catchy, and memorable?

This is the way we spent most of our drive that day: trying to whack ideas out of the tall grass of our imaginations.

"Okay," said Kelly, as she grabbed for a pen and a piece of paper, "Let's start brainstorming."

We came up with twenty or thirty names, until Kelly said, "What about Fedora Pharmaceuticals."

I took my eyes off the road for a split second, craning my neck in her direction. "Where did you get that from?" I asked.

She'd seen our cousin wearing a fedora while we were golfing, and the image had stuck with her. There was something, Kelly insisted, about the shape of a fedora, the circularity of the hat, that had a subtle but powerful symbolism to it. Plus, fedoras seemed to be both old and new at the same time, a relic of a bygone age that had once again gained prominence.

Kelly googled "fedora" and started reading the history of the hat to me as we motored home. Fedoras were especially popular in the early decades of the twentieth century, first adopted by women and then co-opted by gangsters and tough guys. After falling out of favor in the late 1960s and 1970s, fedoras pretty much disappeared until just recently, when they came back into vogue with hipsters and trendsetters.

It was an interesting historical tidbit, but what interested me most of all was how much the general history of fedoras seemed to overlap with the rise and fall of interest in anti-infectives like tazobactam. In the early twentieth century, there was a frantic push to create new antibiotics and anti-infectives. Strides were made, but by the tail end of the century there were so many anti-infectives on the market that doctors started arguing for researchers to turn their attention elsewhere. They figured, naively enough, that modern medicine had conquered these bugs and bacteria for good.

But the misuse and over prescription of antibiotics began to prove that theory wrong, as new superbugs emerged on the scene, many impervious to the drugs currently on the market. And sure enough, everybody was now rushing to fill the void, making anti-infective research hot again.

Fedora Pharmaceuticals. I repeated the word a second time for emphasis to see how it sounded on the rebound. *Fedora Pharmaceuticals.*

Kelly smiled. She liked the way it rolled off the tongue, pinging back and forth between the "f" sound in fedora and "ph" sound in pharmaceuticals.

By the time we got home, I'd already made my mind up. I had a plan—and was fully prepared to do whatever it took to see it through.

CHAPTER EIGHT

Fire and Ice

By early 2010, NAEJA wasn't just awash in debt, it was positively drowning in it. Slashing our rates was no longer a viable long-term strategy. We had a relatively short window of time before we simply ran out of operating revenue.

I was burning through a personal line of credit for hundreds of thousands of dollars—one backed personally by equity from my own home—just to keep NAEJA afloat. Clashes with my family regarding the direction of NAEJA continued, even as I stressed to everyone that we found ourselves in an adapt-or-die situation. I was doing everything I could just to buy time, as the research we had initiated regarding our next-generation beta-lactamase inhibitor was showing real promise.

By this time, our brilliant microbiologist and vice president of business development, Sameeh Salama, was beginning to see real progress in our internal research. One afternoon, he called me into his office and pointed to his computer screen, as he so often did over the course of our twenty-five years together.

"Look at that," he said, "right there."

His finger motioned toward a colorful chart glowing brightly on his computer screen with a set of red, yellow, and green boxes. It was color coded like your typical traffic light. Green indicated positive results. Yellow meant inconclusive. Red was bad news.

When Sameeh compared our compound to other beta-lactamase inhibitors either currently in development or already on the market, including tazobactam, our drug lit up as green as a Christmas tree. It was the equivalent of looking at the stock price of Apple in the early 2000s. All the lines were shooting straight up in the right direction.

Although it would be critical for us to reproduce that data time and again, I knew we were on the right track. As we looked into intellectual property rights and other issues, I flew out to a big anti-infective conference, the Interscience Conference on Antimicrobial Agents and Chemotherapy, to get a second set of eyes on our findings.

We met with Dr. Karen Bush, a noted professor of biotechnology at the University of Indiana. I remember watching Dr. Bush's eyes as they darted left and right across our data. Dr. Bush is brilliant; she fired off questions as she scoured the data while we lobbed back answers to try and keep pace.

Then at one point she grew silent and stopped asking questions. I didn't know quite what to make of it.

Then her intense glare began to melt into a smile. It grew wider, before she put down the data and turned to us.

"I think you guys might really have something here," she said.

We were elated. It was outside confirmation from one of the most well-respected thought leaders in the industry that we might have a compound capable of doing some serious good.

That same month, in September of 2010, I called a special meeting of my family to lay out my vision for how to save NAEJA.

I'd been agonizing over every last detail of my plan for months, mapping out every possible variable and every potential pitfall. The good, the bad, and the potentially ugly. I'd covered it all. I'd counted dollars and cents. I'd worked out investments in terms of hours, timing, and resources. I had my strategy down cold.

It came down to this: I needed to go out and raise angel funds for the creation of a new company, Fedora Pharmaceuticals. Once established, Fedora would acquire NAEJA's new beta-lactamase inhibitor, advance the program, and provide NAEJA a contract to continue its research—thus giving our family's company the capital it so desperately needed to survive.

Meanwhile, on behalf of Fedora, I'd begin contacting large pharmaceutical companies who might be interested in licensing the drug and moving it through human trials. Once the deal was completed, NAEJA would receive a licensing fee (one larger than I was able to get from any other company for such an early-stage program), and Fedora would receive milestones and royalties, rewarding all Fedora investors and NAEJA shareholders alike.

Game. Set. Match. Right?

Not exactly.

When I presented this plan to my family, my words seemed to hang in the air like wisps of air on a cold Edmonton morning. It turned absolutely frigid in that boardroom. First came silence—try to imagine being the target of stares as sharp as icicles—and then a cold, militant opposition to pretty much every idea I'd just laid before them.

The critiques started out slowly and then built momentum. Someone piped up to say it was wholly unacceptable that the Micetich family would not be given equal shares in Fedora. Another family member was baffled by the notion that the Micetich family would not fully control all the seats on Fedora Pharmaceuticals' corporate board.

Even coming from my family, these objections were stunning. NAEJA had been teetering on the brink of bankruptcy for months, and still their sense of entitlement never buckled. They wanted a larger cut of the action and seemed willing to block my whole strategy if they didn't get a larger cut of the future pie.

Hell would have to freeze over, I calmly informed my family, for me to raise angel funds for a new company governed by the very same people who'd run NAEJA.

"On this point," I said, "there is no negotiation."

That opened up a blizzard of new criticisms, all of which were directed at my ability to carry out my plan.

Chris, you don't have the business chops to raise money from angel investors.

Chris, the research isn't promising enough.

Chris, you'll never be able to strike a licensing deal with big pharma.

Chris, you don't know how to run a drug discovery company.

Their negativity was so fierce it was almost overwhelming. After all that had transpired, still no one believed in me.

My response to this doubt?

"You don't think I can do this? Then just sit back and watch me."

My confidence sprung not just from the cold, hard data supporting my compound. Nor from my youthful vigor. Nor from the years of experience I'd spent running SynPhar, DrisCorp, Windjammer, and NAEJA.

No, it came from somewhere different. It came from the inside.

For as much as I still hoped to gain my family's affirmation, I really didn't need it anymore. It was no longer a prerequisite for my happiness or my sense of self-worth.

Through this long and tortuous journey, I'd kicked and scratched and bloodied myself to the point where I honestly felt I was following my own path now. And I knew that I was headed in the right direction. I knew deep down that this was the right course, the *only* course, for NAEJA's survival.

Did I want to make a lot of money? Sure, I did. But there were

> *For as much as I still hoped to gain my family's affirmation, I really didn't need it anymore. It was no longer a prerequisite for my happiness or my sense of self-worth.*

other far more important factors at play, which were audible on the lower frequencies. This push of mine was about moving a drug into development that might save the lives of my children and my grand-children. It was about building a legacy that linked together my work with that of my father. It was about challenging myself to embark on a set of new challenges that lay outside of my comfort zone. In essence, it was an opportunity to see if I could evolve.

And when I sat there, listening to my family scream for handouts and then demand that I cut my salary in half, I think I surprised them all when I responded, "Sure. You can cut my salary in half."

I think, in that moment, the difference between me and my mother and my siblings became crystal clear. Maybe they could see my father shining through me in that moment. Or maybe they just liked the fact that they had pried away yet another concession.

I'm not sure. But I do know that if you want to be a successful entrepreneur, you eventually have to define your own self-worth.

You want trust fund money? You want affirmation from those who've withheld it from you? You want to settle old scores? You want simply to win? Good luck to you, but it's not the same as pursing a path that cultivates self-respect. The key is to feel comfortable about the person staring back at you in the mirror.

All of this became more clear in the wake of an unforeseen tragedy that occurred in early 2011. I had already gone ahead and formally incorporated Fedora Pharmaceuticals, which at that time was just a shell company awaiting investors. I'd been asked by my family to conduct a flurry of last-ditch business trips to keep NAEJA on life support, which I begrudgingly accepted.

My business development partner and I were set to fly out to Europe the next morning, when my phone rang. I picked it up. I listened. And then I almost dropped the receiver in horror when I heard what was happening. One of my best friends, Robert "Teddy" Zack, was in serious trouble.

I'd met Teddy in 2002 while attending one of my son's baseball games. His daughter and my son were on the same team, and we immediately hit it off.

What began as two dads intent on supporting their children's baseball activities turned into a true-blue friendship to the point where I became responsible for christening Rob with his nickname: Teddy.

It occurred to me over dinner one evening, when Rob casually mentioned that he'd never really been graced with a nickname at any point in his life. Because he was as hairy as a teddy bear—with thick tufts of hair that seemed to grow in thickets on his arms—I dubbed my friend "Teddy," a funny moniker that quickly stuck.

On this particular night, however, my friend Teddy was sprawled on the floor of a locker room surrounded by paramedics performing CPR. According to a mutual friend who'd called me, Teddy had suffered a massive heart attack while in the locker room after playing hockey.

Things were not looking good, and my friend indicated that Teddy was about to be transported to a local emergency room at the Grey Nuns Hospital. I hung up, ran to the garage, got in my truck, and sped to the hospital.

Unfortunately, I didn't get there fast enough. As Teddy was a divorcee, there was no one there to look after him at the hospital. There I was, once again pacing an ER waiting room as the life of someone very dear to me hung in the balance.

When the surgeon came out, his eyes dipped to the floor and I knew bad news was coming. He informed me that Teddy had experienced a 99 percent blockage of his left anterior descending artery. There was nothing else they could do. Teddy was gone. The date was June 2, 2011.

I sunk my head into my hands before he even finished his diagnosis. Teddy had no extended family in the area, so it would be up to me, and our mutual friend Jamie, who'd initially phoned me, to drive to his ex-wife's house and inform his two daughters that their father was gone.

It was one of the most difficult moments of my life. Teddy had custody of his children. His daughters saw him as their primary caregiver. He was their life, and they were his.

But it had to be done. So we rang the doorbell and walked through yet another closed doorway that I wish, by some miracle, could have stayed closed.

Teddy's children wept when I told them the news. I wept, too. But in the end, there was nothing I could do for them but tell them how much I loved their father, and how much he loved both of them.

There was so much to do in the aftermath of Teddy's death. It fell on me to oversee the funeral arrangements, and Jamie and I to jointly handled his eulogy. But mostly I just wanted to be there for Teddy's children. I wanted them to know that some part of their dad's life—even if it was just his best friend—was still here, watching over them.

Amid the flurry of activity, I canceled my business trip to Europe. I didn't even think twice about it. Off the calendar it came. And out the door I went to take care of those girls.

My sister Brenda saw things differently. She called my wife, Kelly Alexandra, and began haranguing her over the phone, demanding to know why I wasn't on a plane to Europe at this very moment. Kelly explained the situation, but Brenda was unfazed.

It didn't matter to her. She told Kelly to tell me that I'd better be on the first plane out to Europe in the morning. Kelly, God bless her, didn't wilt in the face of my sister's wrath. She gave it back as good as she got it and told my sister to back off and show some compassion.

The conversation ended with a simple question: "Brenda," my wife asked, "how can you be so utterly insensitive?"

It was there at Teddy's funeral that my mother and my little sister, Debbie, understood the gravity of what had occurred. All they had to do was scan the room and see those girls standing there, alone and afraid, with their tearstained dresses, to realize I'd done the right thing.

After leaning over my best friend's casket to say my final goodbyes, I remember making out the gauzy silhouettes of my mother and sister through the haze of my tears. I could barely see them. But they certainly saw me. And I think they realized, for a single solitary beat, how fragile and fleeting life truly can be.

Things changed in regard to NAEJA after the funeral. My mother and my little sister began actively discussing a potential buyout of Brenda and my brother, Keith, from NAEJA.

But as those discussions heated up, a wholly different but equally unexpected emergency arose one afternoon in July. I'd happened to step out for a quick workout during my lunch break that day, but I can still remember my phone buzzing at the gym and seeing my little sister's name pop up on the display.

On the other end of the line, Debbie didn't even say hello.

"Chris, I think we have a problem; one of the chemists heard a pop and he can smell chemicals. I think we have a problem."

I cut her off and asked her where exactly this was happening—it turned out to be contained to a small lab near one of the storage refrigerators—and then told her to gather our director of chemistry, safety inspector, and maintenance team as quickly as possible.

I was five minutes away from the office, but I managed to get there in two minutes flat.

When I arrived, they were already outside, pointing up at the room that housed the refrigerator. While I was gone, some chemical bottle had broken inside the fridge, releasing a noxious fume so putrid they could smell it throughout the building.

When they'd ventured inside and began looking around, something else had exploded inside the fridge. Flames began flickering to life inside the fridge, batted around by the cold air from the fans inside the refrigerator. Fortunately, everyone had acted quickly and emptied three fire extinguishers on the flames, the smoke from which sounded the alarm. Then they'd gotten the hell out of there.

First I wanted to know if everyone had been evacuated, which they were. My next question focused on whether they'd actually completely extinguished the fire. The consensus was that they had.

It appeared we were in the clear. So we waited for the fire department to arrive. And waited. And waited some more. *What in the world*, I wondered, *is taking the fire department so long to respond?*

It was at that point that I began to see tongues of flames lick their way to life inside the room. Something in the fridge had obviously reignited.

We all stared at that doorway in utter disbelief. Where were those flames going to go? It was unpredictable; the flames began to flow like tiny waves in all directions. And still I looked for some sign of a fire truck. Nothing. No rumble. No siren. No hoses.

My gaze shifted from the window to my watch and back to the streets. The fire was still contained, but valuable time was ticking away. Where were the fire trucks? And still the fire kept kicking out plumes of smoke.

When the firefighters did finally arrive, they informed me that they weren't comfortable going inside. Although the fire was still contained in that one room and could have been easily extinguished, policy dictated that they wait for a dangerous goods team to arrive because of the potential chemicals inside.

And so I watched in horror as the flames continued to chew away at our office. Pale yellow fire grew into a blazing orange carpet. Heat and smoke began flooding out of the window and frosted like black soot over the side of the building. As we waited for the dangerous goods team to arrive, the fire began to burn its way across our entire building.

All that the firefighters would have had to do, from the start, was haul that refrigerator out to the parking lot and it would have been over. Instead, a small fire erupted into an inferno. A perimeter was soon established by the more than eighty firefighters who cordoned off the scene.

I ran over to talk to the fire inspector, only to find a horde of reporters setting up a makeshift headquarters in the building next to ours. As I discussed containment strategies with the fire inspector, the dangerous goods team arrived, but I also saw reporters fan out and begin sticking recorders and microphones in people's faces, interviewing random bystanders on the street.

I knew we were headed somewhere very dangerous now. The people watching the fire from the sidewalk had no idea what had actually happened. They would be offering up pure speculation, so I immediately told the inspector I was going to make a statement to the media.

He grabbed my arm. "Are you sure you want to do that?" he asked, looking at me like I'd completely lost my mind.

"Yes, I am," I told him. "We have nothing to hide. I'll answer whatever questions I can." So I left him there, slack jawed, and walked into the maw of the media circus. I told them exactly what I knew, how the fire broke out, as well as everything they wanted to know about NAEJA.

If you're an entrepreneur and find yourself in the midst of a media firestorm, it's best to take the bull by the horns and control the narrative. Be authentic. Be honest. Stand tall, shoulders straight. Make eye contact. Don't look fragile and weak or uncertain, because your nonverbals will only get magnified on TV. And don't try to apply too much spin, because people have a sixth sense for spotting dishonesty.

I was as open as possible with those reporters, and I wasn't afraid

If you're an entrepreneur and find yourself in the midst of a media firestorm, it's best to take the bull by the horns and control the narrative. Be authentic. Be honest.

to use the bully pulpit to contradict some of the negative stories that had already begun to crop up online and on television. To be honest, I was infuriated with the media when I walked into that ring of fire, because early reports were already calling the fire in our building the second greatest national disaster since the Slave Lake fires, a devastating 2011 blaze that wiped out 40 percent of the town of Slave Lake in Alberta.

It was a pathetic comparison. Not apples to oranges, but apples to watermelons. And yet I've found that nine times out of ten, it's a losing strategy to point fingers. I could have gone on a tirade about the local fire department—how they'd mismanaged, in my opinion, their response to a small fire and turned it into a larger one. I could have walked everyone over to the fifty firefighters who were, at that very moment, munching on pizza as the fire continued to rage. I could have lashed out at the inane bureaucratic red tape that had made things worse.

It was ridiculous, but I didn't let my anger get the better of me. And you shouldn't, either. Take responsibility. Don't try to fight city hall or the authorities or even the press. Quell the fire with honesty; don't fan the flames with vituperation or accusations. And most important of all, don't try to over-explain anything. Keep your words simple, true, and to the point. If you don't know the answer to a question, simply say, "I don't know."

The more technical you get, the more jargon you use, or excuses you throw around, the more that information can be misconstrued and twisted around by lazy journalists. Stick to the facts. And above all, don't make or accept any cell phone conversations if they're within earshot of the press.

A case in point: When my son, who was in high school at the time, caught wind of what was happening, he was concerned about me, so his high school let him call me. When I saw his name come up on my phone, I stepped away from the fray to let him know I was safe.

Somehow a journalist followed me and listened to my discussion over the phone. My son was asking me if I was okay and if I'd lost anything of value. I told him not to worry, the biggest thing I'd lost were my glasses. I was just making a joke, something to ease his mind and try to get him to laugh.

But the next day, one of the small newspapers printed a story indicating that in the midst of the fire my greatest concern was whether my glasses were damaged, twisting my desire to calm my son down into some supreme act of narcissism.

And yet I am 100 percent convinced that had I avoided an interview with the press it would have been a public relations disaster. You know your industry and your company better than anyone else. So leverage that wisdom in times of crisis. If you don't get in front of a story, the media will run with whatever salacious rumors or innuendo will generate the most clicks or best ratings. Step up to the plate and avoid trotting someone else out there. You're the face of the company, so act like it.

That's not to say that when I stepped away from the press things got any easier. When I reconnected with the fire chief, he pulled me aside and said—and I will never forget this— "You don't see what you did very often. Most CEOs I know would have hidden behind a lawyer and issued a press release. I really respect how you handled the situation."

As a result, there was something he felt compelled to show me. He handed me his phone, which contained an email forwarded to him by the Edmonton police force. By this time, my little sister,

Debbie, had joined me. I called her over, and we stared in disbelief as we thumbed down the page.

A letter addressed to Edmonton PD and written under the alias of Frank London was accusing me of intentionally starting the fire. The rambling missive was filled with all sorts of little details that only someone high up within NAEJA could have possibly known.

As my eyes zipped to and fro over the words, anger began to build with each passing lie. Debbie read the text as she stood right next to me, her hand clasped over her mouth in shock.

"Do you know anybody that's out to get you?" asked the fire captain.

I muttered no. Had I fired people in the past? Sure, but no one who would stoop as low as to accuse me of setting fire to my own building. While I tried to think of ex-employees who might have done such a thing, my sister Debbie was more tuned in. She said, "Chris, there is information in this letter that only the board members of NAEJA could possibly know from our closed door discussions. You damn well know exactly who wrote this letter!"

Although I certainly have my strong suspicions as to who wrote that letter, I don't know for certain. The evidence and motive were indeed undeniable and very revealing.

What I do know is that these fabricated allegations could have led to a serious criminal investigation. The lesson? You'll make enemies along the course of your journey. But don't ever underestimate the lengths they'll go to bury you on the way down.

Partners. Friends. Family members. In-laws. It doesn't matter. You can't assume the best from people, even people who are part of your inner circle. Treat your friends like family, but know that your enemies are capable of doing just about anything to bring you down to their level.

Later that night, I couldn't help but marvel at the sight of a bulldozer ripping down a chemical storage vault away from any fire. It was yet another blunder. It likely occurred as the result of a shift change. Wires were crossed. Orders were given to protect part of our space, but it got bulldozed instead, which ensured we would now have a dangerous chemical cleanup to perform we should have never had to deal with.

It was only late into the night that the flames were finally extinguished.

There was something in watching part of our building crumble that really hit home. The fire had wiped away a building block of administrative office spaces, including my father's old office. In time, we'd build a new administrative office on the other side of our lab space, but it was never quite the same.

During the evening following the fire, I kept thinking about all of my father's possessions—those maps, the books, the photographs— and how they must have burned until they melted, bubbling in the heart of the fire, into ash and smoke.

I couldn't help but wonder whether all of my plans for Fedora were burning away right along with them. Was this fire and this evil, fabricated letter all some kind of giant billboard from God telling me to walk away? Or was it one last test? Could this be the final roadblock that I'd have to hurdle to make Fedora a reality?

Things did get worse before they got better. The next day, when online newspaper reports started circulating, I noticed that an individual named Frank London was posting comments underneath the stories, each note accusing me of arson. Debbie called our corporate lawyer, who contacted the papers and told them to remove the blog posts immediately.

At the same time, our internal family struggles intensified. I'd always been hopeful that the relationships within my family would somehow turn from distrust to acceptance. But I'd been wrong. I'd been oblivious to the amount of hatred and jealousy that some members of the family held for me, particularly Brenda and Keith not working in the business.

To my mom's credit, she bought them both out, paying two to three times the value of their shares.

I was finally free, finally able to pursue my Fedora strategy. There was something thrilling in knowing that I was finally at the controls.

Don't be afraid, as an entrepreneur, to motivate yourself through personal narratives. Do what you need to do to feel motivated.

In my case, the storyline was simple: it was Kelly and I against the world.

Don't be afraid, as an entrepreneur, to motivate yourself through personal narratives. Do what you need to do to feel motivated.

It couldn't have been easy for Kelly to come into my life again in 2008. It was Kelly's love that opened the door—literally kicked it open, SWAT style—and made me believe in the prospect of romantic love again. And thus it always bothered me that she never got the love and support from my siblings and mother that I felt she deserved.

It had nothing to do with Kelly and everything to do with my family's feelings toward *me*, and their desire to leverage everything they could to knock me off my pedestal and gain the upper hand.

It's strange, though. The distance we felt from my siblings at family gatherings and parties only brought Kelly and I closer together.

And it was our unity that helped me defy the odds and press forward with Fedora.

The first thing I did when establishing Fedora was rectify the mistake of not getting a unanimous shareholder agreement in place at NAEJA. I created three classes of shareholder. I controlled the vast majority of the class A shares while giving some to my mother and sister for all their support in negotiating the NAEJA buyout and helping to pull it all together. Class B shares would go to my future angel investors, and Fedora's class C shares would be given to longtime employees as well as well as key external advisors.

What was unique about the launch of Fedora was that it was a virtual company. Technically, I was Fedora's sole employee. I'd decided to cap the number of accredited angel investors at fifty to keep things manageable and also meet legal requirements. I didn't want to overplay my hand, having recognized the financial burdens of managing almost fifty-five thousand square feet of finished lab space for NAEJA.

As counterintuitive as it may sound, I believe that sometimes you have to go small to go bigger.

The goal was to earn the trust of an initial set of angel investors so that I could contract the continued chemistry development of the beta-lactamase inhibitor back to NAEJA. When it was time for more biological testing, I could then go raise more money and contract additional research as we moved along.

When you hit the fundraising trail, you have to work on a master narrative. What's your hook? Good data, sound fundamentals, and well-researched projections will seal the deal, but in order to get in the door, you need a compelling story.

Keep it simple. In my case, the master narrative was this: My father's drug, tazobactam, is a $1 billion dollar-a-year anti-infective.

We've come up with something better able to hit the bugs that nothing else can—a twenty-first century drug for twenty-first century antibiotic-resistant bacteria.

That was my pitch, but you have to balance the equation. You need to support that story with evidence. Forget the hard science. Distill everything down to a story they can understand. If you need to draw a comic strip to get your point across, get your pencil out and start drawing.

In the case of our compound, I had to prove to angel investors that big pharma was willing to shell out big money for a compound like the one we were developing.

What I did was point to another anti-infective currently in development and highlight the fact that big pharma had already paid $400 million for the rights to license that drug. This was followed by a slide that showed that our compound was outperforming that $400 million drug in actual studies. All of a sudden we had evidence that a licensing valuation should eclipse $400 million.

You have to be practical—that is, talk dollars and cents—when it comes to investors. They want to know their exit options. What will it take for them to see a profit? And how long is it likely to take? My advice: Give them two or three exit options. Prove that you can steer your way around whatever potential roadblocks might emerge.

Although I was personally invested in getting this drug to the market and saving lives, what my investors really wanted to hear was that they didn't need the drug to actually get approved to turn a profit. All we needed to do was convince a large pharmaceutical company to license it from us at an early stage for the investment to pay off.

In the anti-infective area, the probabilities for predicting success are often visible far earlier than for other drugs. Good animal data correlates very well with good human data. That was worth noting, as it also increased our chances of brokering a license deal quickly.

Once you've delivered your narrative and offered evidence supporting the probability of success, it really comes down to trust. You've got their attention, but do they believe in you? The old Christopher Micetich—the guy so intent on proving himself to his family and his Japanese colleagues—might have stumbled at this point in the process. I might have pressed too hard—rushed the open-look shot, so to speak.

> *Once you've delivered your narrative and offered evidence supporting the probability of success, it really comes down to trust. You've got their attention, but do they believe in you?*

But at this point, my credibility spoke for itself. For over twenty-five years, I'd built up emotional capital and brokered numerous deals with large pharmaceutical companies around the globe. I could close a deal, but I also knew how to run a company. I knew the value of a good board of directors, as evidenced by my ability to wipe the slate clean with the creation of Fedora.

What I did do—and what many entrepreneurs fail to do—is change my presentation after every meeting. Never fall prey to the idea that you have your pitch down cold. I modified my presentation after every meeting based on the questions posed and the responses I gave in return.

Tinker. Twist. Change. Edit. Improve every element of your presentation. In my case, I realized that investors were getting lost when we described what a beta-lactamase inhibitor actually does, so we created a little cartoon to simplify things.

I wanted to make things so clear that anyone who was in the meeting with us could easily relay what they heard to anyone else. I wanted them to be able to go outside and sound like an expert.

Change, as the old saw says, can be a good thing. That being said, never yield to those who want to turn a meeting into a negotiation. I was very straightforward about my position. This was an offering, an opportunity for investors to get in on a great opportunity.

Luckily, the response to our pitches was overwhelming. Most of the fifty angel investors I convinced to invest in Fedora didn't know a lick about science. And maybe only a handful knew anything about infectious disease. It didn't matter. I had the story. I had the data. And I knew how to sell it.

As investors came aboard, one after another, I couldn't help but take pleasure from the fact that I'd pitched this exact same idea to my family. And their response was almost uniformly negative. I remember my sister Brenda saying, "There is no way you're going to convince anyone to invest a single penny in this company."

Fate, it seemed, said otherwise.

CHAPTER NINE

Every Moment Counts

Successful entrepreneurs are, if nothing else, survivors. What's business, after all, but the art of learning how to deflect potentially vicious punches into glancing blows? If you don't have the legs or the self-esteem to absorb one scrape after another—people kicking at your pride, hammering away at your self-worth, bludgeoning your dreams—you're not fit for the game.

In the end, it really does come down to perseverance. Can you get up when everyone is telling you to stay down? Perseverance is about much more than simply enduring; it's about learning.

When I look back at the events that unfolded from 2011 to the close of 2014, I can't help but feel that everything—and I do mean everything—that I had experienced up to that point was meant to happen. The setbacks. The petty jealousies. The family feuds. The losses. The gains.

Everything, in retrospect, feels like it happened for a reason. Is it too cliché in this day and age for me to say that? For me to insist that the razor-thin difference between failure and success often lies in being able to extract wisdom from the hardships that come before?

Academics tell us that history is cyclical—that if you pour over the past with the most powerful of microscopes, you can began to see patterns emerge from the seeming jumble of random events. Time marches on. Backdrops change. Technologies evolve. Conspirators take on different names. Wise men arrive from different lands. But there are lessons to be excavated from days past if we take the time to unearth them.

I can honestly say that I've made as many costly mistakes as shrewd choices, but when I look back at the early years of Fedora, I see a lot of second chances that I was able to capitalize on.

I don't think, for example, that I could have won over my angel investors had I not adopted my father's advice about treating people the right way. Could I have simplified my investment pitches without having spent all those years teaching cupping classes at Windjammer? Probably not. And would I have been able to manage the capital flowing into Fedora as judiciously as I did without all the setbacks I'd experienced at DrisCorp and NAEJA? Definitely not.

Aside from my salary and a single additional employee—my chief scientific officer, Tom—the vast majority of Fedora's capital back in 2011 was being redirected back to NAEJA to keep our research into our anti-infective research humming along.

Had I not experienced the betrayal on the part of Taiho and some of my father's employees at SynPhar, I don't think I would have felt as much loyalty as I did toward my investors. Nor the burning, all-consuming need to make sure I not only returned their kindness but delivered the returns I'd promised.

While my right-hand man, Sameeh, and I were meeting with our angel investors, we'd also opened up talks with twenty-eight major pharmaceutical companies that we felt might be interested in licensing our compound.

We were making progress, until an unexpected obstacle emerged.

Due to a set of complex intellectual property issues, I learned that we were not the sole patent owners of our compound. A Japanese company called Meiji had begun research in the anti-infective arena more than a year before us and had found a way to acquire the global intellectual property rights for what was now our shared drug concept. Fedora, by contrast, controlled the US rights to the same compound.

After parting ways with Taiho in 1999, I'd assumed my days brokering partnerships with Japanese companies had gone the way of the Walkman. With the rights to our potential blockbuster drug now split, however, I had no choice but book a ticket to the East.

Without my prior experience working within Taiho, I wouldn't have known where to start. But thanks to all my years at SynPhar, I knew how to play the game. I knew what to say and when to stay silent. I knew all about the pre-meeting negotiations. The importance of saving face. And the caution that Japanese companies often show in putting a pen to paper.

In order to effectively make a licensing plan with big pharma, I felt I needed to broker a pact with Meiji that would give me bargaining power—that is, both the global and domestic licensing rights for the compound.

If I was to succeed, I had to think like my old mentor Mr. Nakagami. What did we have that Meiji needed?

I asked Sameeh and Tom to look into what percentage of future sales for our compound were likely come from the United States and how much would come from the rest of the world. The data proved to be inconsequential at best.

"Was it 40 percent?"

"No," Sameeh said. "It'll be more than that."

Would it be 80 percent?

"No," he said, "probably not that high."

The magic number, I concluded, seemed to be closer to 60 percent, so I told Sameeh that he had to make me a promise. When we flew off to Japan, we'd have to hammer home, as often as possible, that Fedora Pharmaceuticals stood to gain 60 percent of our joint compound's future sales controlling the US market.

Because Meiji was technically a year and a half ahead of us in studying the compound, its company leaders initially insisted that they didn't need any kind of partnership. Why should they when they were so far ahead of us in development?

I countered with a jab of my own, reminding Meiji that it was Fedora who owned the US rights to the compound. And based on my estimation, the United States represented 60 percent of the world market.

In that moment, the timbre and nature of our conversation changed.

Even though we might have had the upper hand, I didn't want to be greedy. What I wanted was a win-win for both sides. So I approached the rest of the negotiations rationally: if Meiji was ahead of us in research and we held the rights to higher profits, why not just partner together on a fifty-fifty even split?

There was, as is often the case in Japan, hesitation. It was only when Meiji's leadership asked me to estimate the potential licensing fee that this compound could fetch that I won them over. I showed deference, first deflecting the question back to Meiji, who said they estimated about a $5 or $10 million deal.

Leaning forward in my chair, I informed Meiji's leadership that it was my intention to license this compound for—in the very least—nine figures: i.e., hundreds of millions of dollars.

One of Meiji's leaders started laughing and turned to his colleague and said, "I'd really like to see that."

This was my opening. A little silence during a negotiation can have a dramatic effect on who gains control of the conversation. I slowly locked my eyes with everyone sitting around the table, moving from one face to the next, and said, "If we agree on a partnership, I guarantee you we will not sign a deal for less than nine figures."

In that moment, everyone stopped laughing. No more pandering. No more chortles. No more smiles. I was dead serious. And everyone knew it.

Meiji's leadership had a clear choice. Did they want to trust me, this intense Canadian *gaijin*, with wrangling together a contract worth nine figures? Or did they want to settle for their feeble internal projects of $5 to $10 million?

It didn't' take long after that exchange for both sides to agree on a fifty-fifty partnership.

Hurdle number one had been cleared. Before the ink dried, I was already poring over my list of twenty-eight potential suitors, trying to determine who had the capital and interest in our compound to broker a nine-figure licensing deal.

When you start the process of courting high-profile potential suitors, you can't be too picky. You have to listen as much as pitch. Gauge the interest of everyone you can on your list. Be persistent. Some of your emails and meeting requests are going to get lost in the ether. Some phone calls will go unreturned, but keep on pushing.

When you're trying to attract large companies for a major deal, you need to ensure you lay out a clear path as to how they're going to turn a profit on their investment. If we simplified the anti-infective slide for investors, we did the opposite for big pharma. We pummeled them with the hard stuff: the hard science. And then we followed that data dump with a well-constructed development plan as to how they could get this drug to market.

When you start the process of courting high-profile potential suitors, you can't be too picky. You have to listen as much as pitch. Gauge the interest of everyone you can on your list.

We'd previously gone out of our way to conduct discussions with the FDA regarding what the federal government felt was required to get this drug approved. In essence, we'd done some of the work for them already. After all, who doesn't like a bit of a clear runway?

In the beginning, again, you can't be picky. If someone gives you fifteen minutes of their time, take it. We needed to get feedback—any feedback, really—so that we could use it to improve our presentation. Don't be afraid to let people grade you. If someone points out a flaw or struggles with a particular element of your proposed deal, change it for the better.

Don't stick with your initial pitch even if you think you've got it just right.

If a few people stumble over a particular statistical table, go back and make sure you edit that slide to make it as clear and persuasive as possible.

Spend enough time sitting in enough corporate boardrooms and you'll start to develop frames of comparison that tell you who's hungry for what you have and who's more tepid.

Over time, we whittled our list down to our three top choices. Remember the old Micetich rule: *Never go into a negotiation without a backup plan.* You wouldn't invest your family's savings in a single stock, would you? So don't fall in love with one suitor and bet everything you have that they will come aboard. Play a little hard to get, while still keeping your eye on the prize you want most of all.

In our case, our chief target was a leader in the anti-infective space: Roche Pharmaceuticals out of Switzerland. We had initiated term-sheet negotiations with three different companies, but there was something special about the attention that Roche showed me during our initial discussions.

Spend enough time sitting in enough corporate boardrooms and you'll start to develop frames of comparison that tell you who's hungry for what you have and who's more tepid.

Roche's lead negotiator, Vic, exuded professionalism. He was personable, social, and smart as a whip. Vic's lawyer was strict but reasonable. And when we flew out to Switzerland for our meeting, I could see by the number of people on his legal team that Roche was serious about this deal.

We tested their resolve. After flying out to Switzerland and entering into negotiations, we all went out to dinner together. Then, after a few trips where we went to see them, we invited the Roche team to meet us at a conference here in North America. They didn't flinch.

By this time, I realized we were getting serious. Obviously, these were Roche's closers. So I began to build a small, nimble team that I felt could support me as we progressed closer and closer to our goal.

Sameeh, my right-hand man, was overseas, so he couldn't join me. I hired a "leave-no-details-unturned" transactional lawyer out of Boston, Richard Hoffman. He joined me on my trip to Switzerland along with three representatives from Meiji, who had already made it known that I would act as the lead negotiator for both Fedora and Meiji.

On December 5, 2014, my small "special forces" team and I flew out to Switzerland to begin hammering out an initial agreement. I launched into my negotiations with Vic by sticking to what I'd learned while at NAEJA. I didn't waste anyone's time. I laid out our nonstarter sticking points and asked Vic to supply his.

He nodded his head in approval. And the chess match began.

I told him right from the start that I couldn't budge on one thing in particular: I needed a sizable chunk of money up front. This wasn't about me; it was about my angel investors. I knew that the creation of Fedora would not have been possible without the confidence and capital that these investors placed in my company. I felt my number one priority was to fully deliver on the returns that I'd promised them as quickly as possible.

On the plane ride over, a memory had haunted me. It was of my father pulling me into his office during my early months at SynPhar. In my reverie, he was leaning back on his chair, pushing his glasses closer to the bridge of his nose, telling me, "Honor your commitments, Chris. If you make a promise, keep it."

Vic understood where I was coming from. He'd been given authority to finalize a big deal that day, but he'd also been given a cap as to how much money could be shelled out up front. And there was a sizable distance between my number and his.

The negotiations dragged on for hours, in part because our Japanese counterparts stayed silent throughout much of our discussion but would often signal me that we needed to have a breakout session. I was pulling double duty, trying to negotiate in good faith from Meiji's position but also keep the Roche team engaged.

If anything, these breakout sessions sometimes put us in idle just when we were making progress. During one of these timeouts, Vic pulled me aside and said he was glad that I was chief spokesperson for the Fedora-Meiji team, or else he wasn't sure they would continue on.

Tense moments rippled up throughout the course of our talks. There were moments when Roche was ready to walk out the door. And I know for certain there were a number of times that Meiji wanted to call it quits. But I knew we had a unique opportunity here. I'd learned from all the contract deals I'd negotiated on behalf of NAEJA that so much can get lost in translation and culture. I didn't speak Japanese, and no one but the Roche people spoke Swiss, so we had to rely on interpreters to try to decipher the intent behind the words.

Whenever any side became too animated, I saw it as my job to calm everyone down. A successful negotiation has a lot to do with momentum. If a conversation starts veering down the wrong path, who's going to step up and redirect everyone toward the common goal? In international negotiations, pride is a dangerous thing.

Over the course of two nights, we didn't leave the boardroom except to catch a few hours of sleep. It was survival of the fittest. We ate inside the boardroom. We debated inside the boardroom. And finally, we managed to hash out almost all of the most contentious details in that boardroom as well.

I had the authority to sign off on the deal; Vic had the authority to sign off on the deal from Roche. But Meiji's representatives, true to the Japanese style, were unable to sign anything without taking it back to their superiors.

We felt we had a deal brewing, yet there was still some uncertainty as to whether we could iron out some of our differences. We parted ways after two days and returned to our respective headquarters. I don't think I slept more than a couple of hours a night for the next two weeks.

There were middle-of-the-night teleconference broadcasts between Japan, Switzerland, Edmonton, and Boston, my lawyer's home base. Every single second of the day was filled with a flurry of hypotheticals. What if we did X, would Meiji want Y and Roche do Z?

Roche was very clear in its warnings that this deal needed to get done before the December holidays. Should it get bumped into the new year all bets were off, so days didn't just disappear from my calendar, whole weeks seemed to slip away as we brainstormed over every single word in the contract.

We were getting closer, but there was still that fear deep down in the pit of my stomach that someone might be pushed too far. I remember snow being on the ground and greater Edmonton swathed in Christmas lights around that time.

Truth be told, I'd never really gotten over the pain of losing Laura during the holidays. I'd moved past it for the sake of my children and Kelly, but a season filled with joy for most was still fringed with melancholy for me.

I remember lying in bed next to my wife during the early morning hours of December 22, 2014. Kelly was fast asleep next to me. I had my head on my pillow, recounting the day's events. How many nights, over the course of my career, had I spent just like this one, running over and over in my mind what I could have done differently?

All those years spent trying to save SynPhar. The long nights spent pouring coffee beans into giant roasters at Windjammer. All that time spent reeling from the battles between my family and me over NAEJA, trying to figure how to keep my family together.

I flipped over on my pillow and looked over at my beautiful wife, her eyes closed as she escaped into what I hope were less stressful dreams. And as I canvassed my mind for something to regret about this most recent chapter of my life—some turn of phrase, some ill-conceived offering, some misstep—I struggled to come up with anything at all.

Frustrations? Sure, there were plenty of those. But mostly the events that transpired since the creation of Fedora were an entrepreneur's dream, because like Frank (Sinatra, not London) used to say, "I did it my way."

Support at home. A dynamic team. Trustworthy partners and investors. A potential suitor who was as up front and honest as you could possibly want. And a new business—something conceived and executed by me—without the interference of family intent on weighing me down.

I felt—if I can reach for a simple word—fulfilled. When my phone rang, I clicked it on and listened to the voice on the other end.

Okay. Yes. Alright. Okay. That's good. And hung up the phone.

I remember looking at my clock. It read 2:01 a.m.

By this time, Kelly was sitting up, staring at me. She didn't say a word; she just stared. I closed my eyes and laid my head back on the pillow, pretending I was going back to sleep.

"What's going on? What happened?" my wife asked, her eyes bulging with so much excitement they almost popped out of their sockets. *"What ... just ... happened?"*

I opened my eyes and yielded for a pregnant pause. "The document is in; both Roche and Meiji signed it; I'm the last signature that's required to finalize the deal." I said, without a hint of emotion in my voice.

I closed my eyes a second time and pushed my head deep into the pillow.

"What are you doing? You're going back to *sleep*?" Kelly was struggling to even get the words out of her mouth. "You're going back to sleep?"

"Yeah," I said from the comfort of my pillow. "Screw 'em. They made us wait for weeks. Let them wait on *me* this time."

"What are you talking about?" my wife said, now on the brink of total confusion. "You've been waiting for that piece of paper for years. You're going to go back to sleep?!"

I smiled into my pillow and then turned around to look at her with an ear-to-ear grin. "You're right, Kelly," I said, my little ruse now complete. "Damn right! I'm going to sign that document right now!"

We hugged. We kissed. We laughed. It was Kelly and Chris Micetich against the world. And you know what? We'd won.

I raced out of the bed, got to the fax machine at my sister Debbie's house, where the document had arrived, and signed the papers. The $750 million licensing fee between Fedora, Meiji, and Roche was complete, marking the single largest biotech licensing deal in Canadian biotech history.

It was only later that the relevance of the date dawned on me.

December 22, 2014—that was the date I officially signed our deal.

But exactly twenty-five years earlier—on the exact same date, December 22—I'd lost my girlfriend, Laura.

"My god," I said to myself, "What are the odds of that?" But deep down inside, I knew that chance and luck had nothing to do with it whatsoever. What had once been branded into my mind as one of the worst dates on my calendar now became one of the best with the simple stroke of a pen.

CHAPTER TEN

Smash the Glass

After we officially signed off on the Roche deal, I did my best to treat the following morning as if it were just another workday. I got into the office, sat down at my desk, checked over my to-do list, and did what I always do: I got to work.

I felt energized and reinvigorated. Closing a major deal is a stimulant like no other. It makes you feel like you've got an IV of Red Bull coursing through your veins. You want to *go, go, go.*

I was a changed man. Unburdened from the stresses of trying to prove to just about everyone that we could close the deal, I felt more confident in myself, my team, and my vision for the future than I'd ever been in my life. And in the wake of that adrenaline came something quite different: its opposite, a calm that washed over me as gently as a seaborne breeze.

It was heat and peace. Fire and harmony. Invigoration and repose.

At first, I didn't quite know what to make of it. When you spend most of your life trying to prove yourself to others, feelings of contentment, however brief, can raise alarm bells. But that's exactly what I felt the morning after the Roche deal: fulfilled both in my situation and myself for the first time in a very long time.

It was a fleeting sensation, but I knew I wanted more of it in my life. I knew that I'd accomplished something of value—something I did on my own terms, according to my own vision—and yet I still yearned for validation from my family.

Emotional dependence can be an enervating prison to be stuck in. It's a penitentiary of the mind. Looking back, I realized I'd been trapped—like one of those miniature ships encased in a glass bottle— for most of my life. You get used to being trapped for so long that your definition of who you are—and what actual freedom feels like—gets twisted and distorted.

Emotional dependence can be an enervating prison to be stuck in.

I remember running over and over in my mind how things might play out when I formally handed my mom her portion of the up-front signing fee. It was not an insignificant amount. It was a single check larger than anything she had ever seen before, one that set her up financially for the rest of her life. I played out scenes in my head as to how I hoped it would all unfold. By this time, I knew wishing for actual gratitude from my family would be asking for too much. But I kept hoping, in the very least, for some exchange of affection or affirmation. Some signal from my mom that I'd done the job right—that I'd done all right by her and our family. That I'd done something that would've made her and my late father proud. That I'd accomplished exactly what I set out to accomplish.

I imagined the scene. I'd walk over to my mom, pull a check out of my breast suit pocket, and hand it over to her with a bright smile. Maybe she'd nod her head, as if to say in her own silent way, "Good job, Son. You did it." Maybe she'd just look at me, eye to eye, mother to son, with an approving glance. That would have been enough for me.

Only it didn't work out that way at all. When I handed my mother her check, she countered not with approval but by ripping the check from my hand with a stinging question: "So how much did *you* get?"

Maybe I should have known better. Maybe I should have expected less and therefore wouldn't have been so wounded. But I've always been a dreamer—a believer—so there was no reason to assume I'd change now.

I suppose many mothers don't understand just how much power they wield over their children, how little is required, but how much can be achieved. But what did wound me was the realization that my mother was still angry—still oblivious to the work I'd put in, and still holding, tight as a vice grip, to the belief she'd yet to be given the credit she deserved.

In that moment, the glass around me began to crack ever so slightly. I could see the fissures begin to form, because for the first time in my life, I didn't absorb her pain. I reflected it.

I refused to let her emotions dominate mine.

I smiled, and I looked her in the eyes and said, "You're welcome, Mom." And in doing so I began to feel things I'd honestly never felt in my life.

I've got one—and only one—golden rule for entrepreneurs. And that simple maxim is to "know thyself." Self-scrutinize. Self-assess. Look over your life, survey your decisions, and be honest with who you were, who you are now, and who you want to be. That's what this book, this pouring out of my life story, is really all about. Mentors are built not only on the backs of professional success but also through self-actualization and self-scrutiny.

Even after the Roche deal—even after I'd proven to myself what I was truly capable of and gained financial independence for me and my family—I still wasn't free.

The interactions between my family and I didn't get better after the Roche deal; they got uglier. The checks had been distributed. The shareholders, including my mom and sister, got paid and will hopefully continue to get paid for many more years, assuming our drug reaches the market. And initially my life went on much the same as before.

I was still running NAEJA without any family involvement as Debbie had retired shortly after her first Fedora check, with a company line of credit 100 percent backed personally by myself. I was still the president and CEO. Decisions still had to be made. We had another early drug discovery program in the works. And to do it right, I knew I would need, once again, to take enormous amounts of personal risk and money to advance it.

It was a déjà vu all over again. Here I was, in the very same position where I had found myself prior to Fedora. Same stressful situation. Same miasma of doubt. Same internal stressors.

Perseverance and belief had got me to this point in my life. There's little doubt that the Christopher Micetich who had muscled his way past the doubters to sign the Roche deal was forged in the fires of all hardships and family drama that proceeded it. I needed those experiences to become the man I am today, and I remain grateful for them, but did I really need them any longer? Were they still beneficial to my continued growth, or were they stunting me from pushing onward?

This time, I knew things should be different. I had nothing left to prove to myself, or anyone else, for that matter. The weights had been lifted. I had options and insight now—and no desire whatsoever to assume risk and absorb abuse in equal measures.

My family and I needed to part ways—professionally speaking. So in January 2016, I proposed three different scenarios to my mother and little sister, Debbie, the only remaining family members in NAEJA. The options were no different than the ones I proposed to Taiho's leadership years earlier. One: I would buy out my family members' shares. Two: My family members would buy me out. Or three: We would choose to wind it all down, sell the assets of NEAJA and go our separate ways.

Perhaps sensing that I had changed my outlook, coupled with their entitlement issues, poor communication, and incorrect assumptions, my family joined forces to try and ensure that none of the three possibilities became a reality. They called their lawyers; they stopped answering their cell phones and talking to me directly. I was cut off— the severing of the family ties that I had tried so desperately to keep intact for so many years. In an ironic twist of fate, me becoming the reason for them to reunite.

They tried to wield the one weapon they'd always used to cower me. They withheld their love and waited for me to bend.

Only this time, I didn't come crawling back. I decided it was time to smash the glass. It was time to separate family from business at any cost by accepting that the severing of all relations was my path to freedom. I chose not to fight for the money or the company I'd help build. I told my lawyers, "Whatever lingering revenues are left in the company, give them to my mom. Let her have it all."

I could have fought back, but there was no need anymore. It wasn't worth it. By this time, the cracks in the glass all around me had begun to fracture more deeply. Lawyers informed me of the many worst-case scenarios my family could try to concoct and pursue.

"It doesn't matter," I told them, "I will pick my battles and fight for what is right." And the glass split further, ringing, chipping, and splitting even more.

Threats and lawsuits piled up, including attempts to win or scare away some of my staff at Fedora. I ignored them all. We defended what was ours, but no more, as by now bits and sharp shards had already begun to fall away from my glass prison.

Everything changes when you get a little breath of freedom. For far too long, I'd spent every waking moment trying to save NAEJA. I'd devoted myself to saving my father, saving my family, saving the business.

Those days were over. No more *saving*. It was time to devote myself to *creating*.

When I broke free of NAEJA, I shattered the glass, free and clear. I was the same Christopher. Same man. Same drive. Same values. Same ambitions. But with liberation came a newfound freedom to pursue new opportunities on my own terms.

The first thing I did was take care of the people who stood by me over the years. Much of the time I'd spent trying to please my family in the past was now reallocated toward spending more time with my wife and children. I took care of my employees as well, hiring a team who stood with me for many years and creating a new company called Brass Dome Ventures.

> *The first thing I did was take care of the people who stood by me over the years.*

My principle motivation for launching Brass Dome was to keep my employees together and to give them a hint of the same security that Kelly and I now felt. We certainly didn't need to do anything after NAEJA. I could've retired. My wife and I could've gone and done whatever we wanted to do, but I felt a deep and abiding obligation to my team. Call it a debt paid, proof that I am my father's son.

Brass Dome Ventures became the public face of Fedora. Currently, all of our staff at Fedora is under a master service agreement with Brass Dome. We're building a drug pipeline for Fedora and representing the company internationally.

In May of 2016, Kelly and I bought an office building in downtown Edmonton. Kelly renovated it to ensure it reflected who we are and what we believe. Thanks to her efforts, it is a stunning place to go to work. And, for the first time, we have a company that's completely ours.

There was a pang of discomfort that came along with making these new memories. I thought a lot about my dad when I moved into my new office. And I couldn't help but think about my family as well.

Despite all the things that Kelly and I have endured, I still miss them. If we could find a way to reconnect in a healthy way, I'd be overjoyed. They will always be an integral part of my story, but at Brass Dome Ventures, with my wife at my side, I feel more liberated than ever. The harder, rougher edges of the old Christopher have slowly sloughed away, leaving me closer to the man and entrepreneur I've long wanted to be.

I realize that everyone has their own individual definition of freedom. Some people seek financial freedom, others the freedom of time to live their life, moment to moment, according to their own schedule and passions.

Both of these freedoms are laudable pursuits, but I think I've found something greater—an even more rewarding freedom. I have been blessed with the freedom of purpose, which is the ultimate freedom, because it encapsulates all of the above, including the freedom of relationships.

I've got my own "family" by my side now. These are—and have always been—the believers. And so now, as we continue to pursue new pharmaceutical deals, I've committed myself to helping other entrepreneurs pursue their professional goals and dreams.

We want to invest in other people and other companies. We perform business evaluations. We consult. We seek not just to mentor as a verb, but to be mentors as nouns.

Our clients come from all walks of life. Some are old; some are young. Some seek financial freedom; some seek peace of mind. Some want to build new businesses; some want to preserve them.

I still believe, now more strongly than ever, that people matter. Show respect and you will receive it tenfold in return. My father. Laura. My team. My wife. They all taught me that lesson. I try to impress that rather simple but incredibly important fact on my clients. But I also make it known to everyone I speak to that their own stories—the pain and glories of their respective histories—matter as well.

I still believe, now more strongly than ever, that people matter. Show respect and you will receive it tenfold in return.

I can offer them plenty of practical advice about how to negotiate a deal, how to raise funds, how to run a family business, and the importance of unanimous shareholder agreements. But in the end, I always come back to the idea that self-reflection is indispensable—that sometimes freedom is the result not of absorbing the answers from outside parties but of mining your own history and stories for what you know to be true but have difficulty facing.

"Do the things," I tell them, "that you don't like doing."

Sometimes, after a successful consultation, after we've helped our clients change the course of their businesses—and in some cases their lives—they will ask me how I got to be in the position I'm in, why I continue to be an entrepreneur and consultant when I could be doing anything in the world.

My response is always the same: "Let me tell you a story," I tell them, "It involves a guy from Canada—Sherwood Park, Alberta, to be exact—who believed in a product, a business, a set of ideas and values, when everyone around him doubted."

EPILOGUE

At this point in my life, I find myself—as fate often has it—as the mentor, not the mentee, the father figure rather than the pupil. I'm sitting on the opposite side of the desk. I'm in the big comfy chair now, sitting behind the big desk, only this time, views of downtown Edmonton stretch out in the distance over my shoulders.

While my father liked to work in a confined space, homey and familiar, I like the reach and expanse of our new offices that my wife, Kelly, my team, and I have built in the heart of Edmonton. I don't have to peak through walls of paperwork the way my father did. I swivel around in my chair, eyes focused on my computer screen, as data streams in and the web takes me wherever my thoughts are leading me for the day.

Now I can hear the bullet train coming from across the room— my first born, Brendan—barreling toward my office. He's not as tall as me, but he's built like a Hummer. Full sleeve tattoo. Athletic build from years of playing hockey and lifting weights. The look and air of confidence that could land him a contract as a fitness model.

He's polite and kind—probably more so than I was at his age—and he has a great sense of humor. I tell him his hair is thinning up top, and he tells me to go look in the mirror.

Not to mention the kid has ideas to spare. When I hear him thundering toward my office, I know where he's going to land: in one of the four chairs I've set up around a large table in my office.

He's been with me since the launch of Brass Dome Ventures, and he hasn't been shy about voicing to me what he thinks we should focus on, just as I wasn't with my father a generation ago. He's got interesting ideas, especially on how to leverage next-generation social media channels, to set Brass Dome up for long-term success with young and up-and-coming entrepreneurs.

Most days I hear him coming, I realize I don't really have the time to sit and discuss his latest brainstorm, but then I think of my own father and how he always found time, so I make sure to do the same.

So I let him talk—and I listen. Whenever he runs out of steam, I try to teach him, in my own way, what my father was trying to teach me when I was his age. The truth is that I've devoted a great deal of time to thinking about the idea of mentor as a noun rather than a verb, and these father-son moments are a means for me to put my theories into action.

While my father asked me to simply observe and learn, I've discovered the value of cloaking my wisdom in story form. I believe a spoonful of storytelling helps the medicine go down. I don't tell my son what to do, but I do tell him what I did—whether it was decades ago or a week prior—and why I did it. And *then*, I go silent.

I know this much to be undoubtedly true: You can't tell an entrepreneur what they shouldn't be doing—or God forbid, exactly what they should do. The key is to try to identify what they need to learn. You ask them questions. You let them answer. And then you tell them a story—a good story, one that's pertinent to them and their situation.

So I let my son, in his own way, figure out what parts of my story overlap with his. I hand over the stories to him and give him time to process them. I want him to find his own wisdom in them. Being a former teacher, I want him to claim his own discoveries and own them, so that I can disappear into the background, well aware of the impact I've made and the effort he has poured into the experience himself.

I hope this book and stories within it have helped you, the reader, find your own truths—in your own personal and professional life— whatever they may be, and that you use your wisdom as a mentor to pay it forward to those in your circles who need it most.

I can honestly say that some of the most rewarding moments in my office have been when I've seen the light bulb flicker on over my son's head as he found his way toward a solution that seemed out of reach only moments earlier. And yet there are some aspects of my story that remain outside his reach, waiting only for time and experience to make clear.

I know that look on his face when I see it, because I had that same look when I was his age. I always think of my father in moments like these, and I can't help repeating that old phrase delivered to me many times over the years.

"One day," I tell my son, smiling my father's smile. "You'll understand, son. One day you will truly understand."